FILIPINO
MARTIAL ARTS
Exploring the Depths

FILIPINO MARTIAL ARTS

Exploring the Depths

Peter A.H. Lewis

Foreword by Grandmaster
Reynaldo S. Galang

THE CROWOOD PRESS

First published in 2016 by
The Crowood Press Ltd
Ramsbury, Marlborough
Wiltshire SN8 2HR

www.crowood.com

British Library Cataloguing-in-Publication Data
A catalogue record for this book is available from the British Library.

ISBN 978 1 78500 157 4

Dedication

To my parents Jean and Harry Lewis for the life that you have given to me and for the many years of sacrifice and guidance that have helped me to become a better person. To my teachers in the Filipino martial arts, Grandmaster Epifanio 'Yuli' Romo and Grandmaster Reynaldo Galang for providing my journey with depth, understanding, knowledge and endless enjoyment. To the late Grandmaster Christopher 'Topher' Ricketts, your friendship, guidance and support have enriched my journey greatly and will continually inspire me. To my wife Jenny and daughters, Marisa and Verity, your love and support are a constant source of inspiration to me. To my students who constantly strive to guard the legacy of the art and for being a source of constant motivation.

Acknowledgements

Special thanks to training partners David Hand, Kevin Jones and Audrey Tyler for sharing the journey and keeping me motivated to explore creatively the Filipino martial arts. Deep appreciation to my teacher in the Filipino martial arts, Grandmaster Reynaldo Galang, for your considerable encouragement and support in writing this book. Respectful gratitude to my students, David Hand, Kevin Jones, Audrey Tyler, Jade Tyler and Jamie Orgee for sharing their technical expertise and support in the photographic content of the book. A huge thank you to David Hand and Marisa Lewis for the excellent photographs that are used throughout, with a special acknowledgement to Marisa for taking the cover photos. Finally, sincere appreciation to Kevin Jones, Verity Lewis and Sarah Littlehales for proofreading the manuscript.

Disclaimer
The author and publisher of this book are not responsible in any manner whatsoever for any loss, damage, injury or any other adverse consequence of any nature that may result from studying, practising or applying any of the concepts, techniques or ideas and/or from following any information or instructions contained within this publication. The practice of martial arts techniques can be dangerous and too strenuous for some individuals to engage with safely and it is absolutely essential that a doctor be consulted prior to commencing such practice.

Typeset by Sharon Dainton
Printed and bound in India by Replika Press Pvt Ltd.

CONTENTS

A range of weapons used in the Filipino martial arts.

FOREWORD

A more appropriate title could not exist for this book on the Warrior Arts of the Philippines, better known as Filipino Martial Arts (FMA), than *Filipino Martial Arts: Exploring the Depths*. Known to and embraced only by select and discriminating members of the military, police and combative practices, the Filipino Martial Arts continue to grow in popularity throughout the world.

In aptly heralding the characteristic of this art with this intriguing title, Peter Lewis has indicated the many facets that are the striking peculiarity of this art. FMA is best described as learning characterized not by accumulation, but by accretion. Each layer of technique and knowledge is a contributing and reinforcing variation, application and simplification of past elements learned. As knowledge and experience is amassed, the elements become simpler, more efficient, more natural and instinctive. From mastery of weapons to simple and brutal empty hand applications, FMA develops a distinct persona within the practitioner.

In this book, Peter Lewis takes the reader by the hand and shares the many epiphanies he has encountered in his odyssey through these unique martial arts. Having learned, mastered and analysed the art, Peter unveils the many layered secrets, attributes and riches of this treasure trove known as Filipino Martial Arts.

I am pleased that Peter Lewis has taken the time and effort to write this book to record, preserve, and expose the Filipino Martial Arts as seen through the eyes of a dedicated disciple, practitioner and teacher.

Reynaldo S. Galang
Bakbakan International WHQ
Grandmaster – Bakbakan Kali
Canberra, Australia

PREFACE

This book is written with the intention of providing the reader with an opportunity to share in a journey of exploration and discovery of the Filipino martial arts that are generally known as *Arnis, Arnis de Mano, Eskrima, Escrima* or *Kali,* among other variants. I hope that it will encourage and inspire creativity, understanding and a deep exploration of techniques, translations and applications regardless of the system practised. The techniques and terminology used as a vehicle for investigation are from the *Bakbakan Kali* system as taught by Grandmaster Reynaldo Galang. Many techniques will be familiar regardless of the system studied and some may be new, but the overall purpose is to explore personal practices and methods and discover creatively the potential within the Filipino martial arts.

Friends and colleagues within the Filipino martial arts community will appreciate the vast expanse of knowledge available and the endless diversity of potential applications and translations of moves generally first practised with a weapon. It is way beyond the scope of any book to convey the plethora of opportunities contained within our arts and that journey of discovery is ultimately very individual and part of a lifelong pursuit.

The book focuses on two main and fairly generic aspects of the Filipino martial arts. The first section explores the twin weapon aspect widely termed as *sinawali* and that usually begins with the use of two sticks or *doble baston.* Consideration is given to fundamental, intermediate and advanced techniques within this category and the evolution of the system to embrace other weapons and devastating empty-hand application. The second section investigates and explores the use of a single stick known as *solo baston.* A detailed overview of fundamental, intermediate and advanced techniques within this group is provided, together with the identification to translate methods to other weapons classifications or to empty-hand scenarios.

The concluding chapter sets the path to a continued exploration and identifies some opportunities for further study of the Filipino martial arts. The framework of analysis and exploration is expanded to identify the route to ongoing discovery and evolution. I hope that you enjoy your journey within the Filipino martial arts, regardless of the system studied.

Peter Lewis
August 2015
Worcester, England

INTRODUCTION

The Filipino martial arts (FMA) are revered and respected worldwide for the development of a deep understanding of defensive strategies against impact and edged weapons and empty-handed combative attacks. The martial practices of the Philippine archipelago are known by a range of different names, including *Arnis, Arnis de Mano, Eskrima, Escrima* or *Kali* among others. These differences will not form the focus of this book and are seen as peripheral to the task of exploring the plethora of opportunities available within these unique martial arts. The distinctive training methodology adopted within the Filipino martial arts is the reverse of most of the counterparts from other countries in that training generally begins with the use of a either an impact or bladed weapon. This practice facilitates an early and immediate appreciation of strategies, concepts and techniques that are appropriate to defending against such weapon-based attacks. The methodology further enhances the necessary attributes for effective self-protection applications such as mobility, speed, focus, accuracy, timing, adaptability, destructive power, explosiveness and mental agility.

Exploring the Depths

The martial arts of the Philippines are often described as a 'conceptual' or 'thinking' martial arts, developing advanced skills and the ability to analyze, evaluate and adapt within an endless variety of combative situations. This high-level analytical development is central to the purpose of this book to explore the Filipino martial arts in a greater depth and to encourage practitioners to look beyond the obvious physical techniques as they progress and evolve on their own journey of understanding and creativity. Throughout the book, a technical overview of each technique is provided, solo and partner-based development opportunities using equipment are identified and translations to other weapon categories and empty-hand scenarios are explored. Far from being exclusive, exhaustive or prescriptive, the purpose of such detail is to encourage an open-minded and creative approach that will become unique to each individual practitioner as they focus on their individual needs.

Weapons Categories

The Filipino martial arts are renowned for the development of effective and efficient defensive and offensive strategies with and against a diverse range of weapons or empty-hand scenarios. Once proficient in the core elements of these dynamic and destructive martial arts, the practitioner can feel a degree of confidence in using almost any implement as a weapon. With this unique adaptability it can be difficult to categorise such a myriad of opportunities and this is not the purpose of this book. To provide a broad

De Cuerdas (rebounding moves) using double sticks.

De Cuerdas (rebounding moves) without weapons.

understanding of common classifications, weapons could be grouped into four main types to incorporate projectile weapons, flexible weapons, impact weapons and edged weapons. There may be sub-divisions with each classification that further define the overall scope of the Filipino martial arts. Projectile weapons may include *barya* (coins), *bato* (stones), *siit* (twigs) and a *sibat* (spear) that can be projected through the bodily mechanics and physicality of the practitioner. Other projectile weapons depend less on the physical attributes of the proponent but rather make use of equipment to enhance the delivery, generally in a more forceful manner. Some examples within this category can include a *tirador* (catapult or slingshot) and *pana* (bow and arrow or crossbow). The second group of weapons are those of a flexible nature and can include the *panyo* (handkerchief), *bandana* (scarf), *Lubid* (rope), *kadena* (chain) and *tabok-toyok* (flails). The next group of hand-held weapons possesses a hard surface and are classified as impact weapons. While not exclusive, this group contains a variety of sticks employed by the Filipino martial artist. Within this group are sticks made of rattan cane, *bahi* (palm) or *kamagong* (mahogany or iron wood) and weapons can include the commonly used *baston* (rattan cane of 710mm to 812mm in length), *tungkod* (short staff of 910mm to 1,200mm in length) and the *dulo-dulo* (pointed carabao horn or kamagong short stick of approximately 150mm in length). The final group of weapons are edged or bladed

weapons. This category is vast within the Filipino martial arts and includes a diverse range of single and double-edged swords and knives. Some examples of swords employed within this classification include the *kampilan* (long single-edged cutlass with a 635mm long blade), *ginunting* (a beak-shaped sword with a 500mm long blade), *sansibar* (a slightly curved sword with a blade length of 538mm) and the *barong* (a leaf-shaped sword with a 380mm blade length). Some of the knives within the edged weapon category include the *kerambit* (a curved or hook-shaped short blade), *balisong* (folding butterfly knife) and the *baraw* (dagger).

Use of Supportive Equipment

The development of combative techniques that are readily available at an instant requires time, dedication and focused effort to achieve. This process can be supported greatly through the use of a variety of equipment to provide focused enhancement of the various key attributes that collectively result in the improved delivery of the motion. This book will explore and incorporate equipment to focus on impact power, accuracy of movement, muscular strength development and accuracy with power in a more dynamic scenario. The development of impact power will be explored by using the heavy bag or a section of heavy shipping rope

Use of a mirror to develop accuracy.

Striking the heavy rope to develop impact power.

Using metal bars to develop strength.

as a target for full power striking. Accuracy of movement can be greatly enhanced by performing the technique in front of a mirror at a slow speed to ensure correct alignment and trajectory at each phase of the technique. Developing muscular strength throughout the entire technique can benefit from its performance using metal bars, which gives the added benefit of increasing essential grip and wrist strength. Finally, developing fast, powerful and accurate techniques that can be applied in a more dynamic and combative situation can be improved during partner training with the use of focus mitts that are randomly presented as targets.

A Word on Weapon Alignment

As techniques evolve and delivery is performed with increased speed and power, it is essential to avoid injuries or loss of the weapon by maintaining structural alignment and stability throughout the entire movement. This is of particular importance during the execution of striking techniques and is best achieved by leading with the middle knuckles of the weapon hand to ensure blade alignment, even when performing the motion with a stick. The adoption of this practice not only enhances the structure of the technique but more readily supports the translation of performance from impact weapons to edged weapons with minimal modification of delivery.

Points of Reference

Throughout the book a technical description of each technique is provided and directional movements identified. To support this descriptive element of the exploration, the reference points of *abierta* (open) and *serrada* (closed) are adopted. *Abierta* is an open position where, for example, if the weapon is held in the right hand then the starting point or chamber is also on the right side of the body. Conversely, *serrada* is a closed position where the weapon is held across the body, for example with the weapon held in the right hand the chamber or starting position is on the left side of the

---

BAKBAKAN INTERNATIONAL – RAISING THE STANDARD

Bakbakan International is a brotherhood of martial arts practitioners that was founded in the late 1960s by the late Grandmaster Christopher 'Topher' Ricketts and early members included Ding Binay, Rolly Maximo, Christian Gloria, Eddie Alicante, Rey Vizer and Reynaldo Galang among others. Bakbakan International is a place for sharing of knowledge, developing skills and testing ability through full-contact sparring and the constant analysis of combative methods. This elite organization maintains a strong commitment to propagating and enhancing the Warrior Arts of the Philippines through the constant efforts of a select and dedicated group of practitioners. Enjoying a long and well-established relationship with the late Grandmaster Antonio 'Tatang' Ilustrisimo, the techniques, concepts, strategies and training methods of *Kali Ilustrisimo* feature strongly in the repertoire of methods adopted by Bakbakan International. Dominant systems taught within Bakbakan International include:

- *Kali Ilustrisimo* as taught by the late Grandmaster Christopher Ricketts.
- *Bakbakan Kali Ilustrisimo* as taught by Grandmaster Reynaldo S. Galang.
- *Tulisan* Knife System which is an offshoot of the *Kali Ilustrisimo* system.
- *Bakbakan Sinawali* which is a highly structured and advanced system of double weapon methods systematised by Grandmaster Reynaldo S. Galang.
- *Sagasa* Kickboxing System founded by the late Grandmaster Christopher Ricketts.
- *Hagibis* Grappling System founded by Grandmaster Reynaldo S. Galang.

Bakbakan International Group. (Photo: Reynaldo S. Galang)

Bakbakan International Logo. (Photo: Reynaldo S. Galang)

Weapon alignment when using a sword.

Weapon alignment when using a stick.

High abierta (open) position.

Low serrada (closed) position.

body. Additionally, there can be a high (shoulder height), middle (stomach height) or low (waist height or below) points of reference. These standards are used to provide greater detail of the starting point, directional movement and the conclusion of techniques that may be less obvious in a photographic representation.

Terminology

The indigenous martial arts of the Philippines are present throughout the archipelago and have many influencing factors, including the use of terminology to describe or name techniques. With such a diverse range of local and regional dialects all having a bearing on the many systems of Filipino martial arts there is a need for clarity, simplicity and structure in presenting the techniques explored in a manner that is accessible to enthusiasts. It is not the intention of this work to present a system-specific overview but rather an approach to exploring in greater depth the diversity, complexity and sophistication of techniques regardless of the system practised by individuals. The terminology used throughout this book is that applied in the Bakbakan Kali Ilustrisimo system as taught by Grandmaster Reynaldo S. Galang. This selection is to facilitate a simple reference

for the movement or combination of moves and to avoid the confusion of presenting the many available names for the same technique.

Structure of Subsequent Chapters

The remainder of this book is presented in two specific sections that explore the fundamental, intermediate and advanced techniques of the *sinawali* (twin weapons), which is generally practised using *doble baston* (double sticks), and *solo baston* (single stick) components of the Filipino martial arts. An initial overview of each technique is presented and includes details of the structure and alignment of each motion applied. This is followed by an exploration of solo and partner-based training methods that can enhance the development of the technique in relation to accuracy, speed, power and functionality in a combative scenario. Finally, opportunities to translate the technique to other weapon categories and empty-hand methods are identified and presented in a non-exhaustive manner with a view to unlocking the potential for further discovery throughout the practitioner's journey.

SINAWALI

The Filipino martial arts have many facets but perhaps the most impressive from the spectator viewpoint is that of *sinawali* (to weave or the pattern without patterns), or the use of twin weapons. The blur of rapid motion and the sound of *doble baston* (double sticks) clashing is captivating, dynamic, inspiring and mesmerizing. The practice of using double sticks not only facilitates the progressive development of enhanced co-ordination, but develops the naturally weak side of the body considerably while giving the practitioner advanced combative skills and strategies. An aspect that is less obvious to the onlooker is the natural ability to translate the techniques of *sinawali* into other weapon categories, such as the more advanced combinations of e*spada y daga* (sword and dagger) or *kalis kaluban* (sword and scabbard). These advanced combinations enable the refinement of timing and range adjustment while moving from long to short weapon usage. Of great benefit to the practitioner of *sinawali* is the development of advanced and complex empty-hand skills through the adaptation of the stick movements. Through the analysis of the stick motions practised in *sinawali*, the exponent acquires the ability to block, parry, smash, destroy, deflect, redirect, lock or manipulate in a fast, fluid, explosive and highly effective manner.

Baguhan using double sticks.

Baguhan using the short staff.

Baguhan using empty hands.

SINAWALI

This section of the book will explore some of the fundamental, intermediate and advanced methods of *sinawali* that are found in many systems of the Filipino martial arts. Within these three groups of techniques, a technical overview of each method is provided together with the identification of opportunities for development through individual and partner-based training methods. Finally, opportunities to translate techniques across weapons categories are investigated and adaptations to empty-hand methods are examined to provide the reader with a greater understanding of the scope of this fascinating component of the Filipino martial arts.

CHAPTER I

FUNDAMENTAL TECHNIQUES OF SINAWALI

The importance of developing strong basic techniques is often conveyed during the martial arts journey by those who started before us. Within the Filipino martial arts, where training often involves the use of impact or bladed weapons, developing the fundamental techniques is especially important. This chapter will provide a clear and detailed overview of the fundamental techniques of double weapon training, known generally within the Filipino martial arts as *sinawali*. Common to most systems of the indigenous martial arts of the Philippines, *sinawali* is used as an early vehicle with which to develop excellent coordination skills with both sides of the body. In more advanced practice, *sinawali* develops highly effective combative skills, both with and without weapons and can easily be viewed as a complete martial art in its own right. With a focus on the basic downward X, upward X and C striking patterns, this chapter will outline the background, structure and development of each technique, as well as provide options for the translation of skills to other weapon categories and empty-hand defensive strategies.

Magbabayo – To Pound – Downward 'X'

One of the most basic techniques from the double weapon category is the simple downward X motion, which is known by various names but for the purpose of this review is termed *magbabayo*. Derived from an agricultural application, the term *magbabayo* depicts the motion of a farmer using a large mortar and pestle to pound grains of rice. The strong action of smashing down with the pestle to crush the rice in the mortar is mirrored in both intent and structure when performing this most fundamental of *sinawali*

techniques. While a very powerful technique in its own right, magbabayo is the foundation for the intermediate techniques of *redonda* (whirlwind) and *bukang liwayway* (sun rays) and the more advanced *sinawali* techniques of *luha redonda* (teardrop thrusts with whirlwind) and *pluma bukang liwayway* (pen defence with sun rays).

Structure and Mechanics

Magbabayo comprises two diagonally downward strikes using the same weapon. The first strike starts from the *abierta* (open) side at shoulder height and travels diagonally downwards to the *serrada* (closed) side to hip level. The second strike commences from the *serrada* side at shoulder height and progresses diagonally downwards, ending on the *abierta* side at hip level. Leading with the second knuckles to

Magbabayo first move.   *Magbabayo second move.*

maintain a blade orientation, the first strike has the palm of the hand diagonally upwards towards the *serrada* side and the second strike, also leading with the second knuckles, has the palm diagonally downwards towards the *serrada* side. Power is generated by using full hip twisting during the execution of *magbabayo*. The first strike is preceded with a sharp and slightly downward twist of the hips towards the serrada side of the body to accelerate the striking motion of arm and weapon. Just prior to the second strike, the hip motion is reversed to twist slightly downwards towards the *abierta* side of the body, again accelerating the motion of the arm and weapon to generate power.

Methods of Development

Structured and progressive training are the roots of developing techniques that are powerful, accurate and can be applied instantly as required. This is never more essential than with the evolution of the fundamental methods of *sinawali*. With a focused and structured approach, core attributes, such as coordination, functionality, fluidity, timing, grip and wrist strength, impact power and accuracy can be developed. Training methods to support the development of *magbabayo* can include solo methods or those that use the support of a training partner. Both formats offer the essential ingredients for the overall development of the technique.

The first solo training method is the use of a large diameter stick for grip and wrist strength development. In this training method the *magbabayo* technique should be performed deliberately slowly to support the development of strength throughout the entire motion. It is important to ensure that the technique is structurally stable and this is achieved by leading with the middle knuckle of the hand to simulate a blade alignment.

A second solo training method used to develop strength and impact power in the *magababayo* technique is to strike a heavy bag. This training method is excellent for the development of precise body mechanics and technique alignment while striking at full power. Care should be taken when striking at full power because poor alignment could result in wrist injuries. When executing *magbabayo* on the heavy bag, full use of hip twist should be applied as well as leading

with the middle knuckles for blade orientation during the strike. Impact should be made with the top portion of the stick.

Partner-based training methods allow magbabayo to be developed against a moving target for accuracy as well as to gain a deeper understanding of how the technique can be applied. The first and most basic

Magbabayo using a large diameter stick.

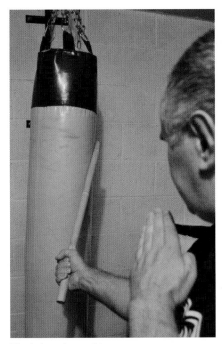

Magbabayo bag striking.

Magbabayo striking with the same stick.

Magbabayo using focus pads.

partner training method is where both practitioners strike *magbabayo* using the same stick. In this method, the right stick will strike the partner's right stick and the left stick will strike the partner's left stick. This method is very effective in developing range appreciation, blocking skills and the feel of correct alignment when making impact.

Another partner-based training method is to have the partner wear focus mitts and present random, pad up targets to enable the development of accurate and powerful strikes against a moving target. This method develops very good range adjustment and appreciation, as well as accuracy and timing in executing *magbabayo*.

Translation to Other Weapon Categories

As a fundamental technique from the *sinawali* (double weapon) category, *magbabayo* is very flexible and translates readily to applications with other weapons. The first translation to be considered is to perform *magbabayo* using a sword. This method develops a high degree of accuracy of performance as well as being very much associated with the backbone of many Filipino martial arts systems. Until a high degree of skill is developed, *magababayo* should be performed deliberately slowly to ensure the integrity and accuracy of the technique, leading at all times with the middle knuckles or cutting edge of the sword.

A second option for translating *magbabayo* is to use a *tungkod* (staff), which provides the scope to perform the technique with a double-handed grip. If

Magbabayo using the short staff.

striking from the right side of the body first, the *tungkod* is held at one end in a two-handed grip with the right hand highest and facing palm up. The left hand is below the right hand and is facing palm down. The execution of *magbabayo* should be structurally sound by leading with the middle knuckles of the hand in a blade alignment and should make full use of body twisting to develop power throughout the move.

Translation to Empty-Hand Applications

As a core fundamental technique, *magbabayo* is both fast and powerful, and can be translated readily into the empty-hand category. The technique can be used to block, parry, redirect, control or strike in a wide variety of scenarios. The first application is to apply *magbabayo* against an attempted grab technique using the forearm as the striking weapon. Assuming a

Magbabayo using the barong sword.

Magbabayo against a grab.

Magbabayo against a grab.

direct it firstly to the left in a right abierta to right *serrada* downward diagonal direction. Suddenly change direction by taking the head in a right *serrada* to right *abierta* downward diagonal direction and into a right knee strike to the face.

Salok-Saboy – To Scoop and Throw – Upward 'X'

Another of the more fundamental techniques from the *sinawali* category is the upward X pattern, which has a variety of names but for the purpose of analysis is known as *salok-saboy*. The term, which also originates from an agricultural technique, means to scoop and throw and describes the motion of a farmer scooping seeds from a bucket and throwing them on to the ground. This smooth and fluid action of the farmer sowing seeds is an essential attribute of the efficient application of the salok-saboy technique. While a very useful technique, especially for countering downward attacks, *salok-saboy* is the foundation of the intermediate *sinawali* techniques of *redonda salok-saboy* (reverse whirlwind) and *de cuerdas* (rebounding strikes). *Salok-saboy* further supports the evolution of skills towards the advanced *luha redonda* (teardrop thrusts with whirlwind) and *luha salisi* (criss-cross thrusts).

Structure and Mechanics

Salok-saboy uses the same weapon to execute two diagonally upward strikes. Starting from the *abierta* (open) position at hip height, the first strike travels diagonally upwards to shoulder level on the *serrada* (closed) side of the body. The second strike begins at hip level on the *serrada* side and moves diagonally upward to finish at shoulder height on the *abierta* side. Structurally, the first strike leads with the second knuckles, with the palm diagonally up towards the *abierta* side. The second strike also leads with the second knuckles and has the palm diagonally downwards, pointing towards the *abierta* side of the body. Power is generated by twisting the hips during the execution of the *salok-saboy* technique. The first strike is preceded by a sharp and slightly upward twist of the hips towards the *serrada* side of the body. Similarly, the return strike commences with a sharp

right lead stance, as the attacker attempts to make a right lapel grab, smash into their inner forearm with a right *abierta* to right serrada strike using the little finger side of the forearm. This powerful *gunting* (limb destruction) technique is followed immediately by a second strike travelling from right *serrada* towards right *abierta* and using the little finger edge of the forearm to strike the attacker's right collarbone area or right side of the face.

The second translation of *magbabayo* into the empty-hand category is to apply it at medium to close range as a grappling technique to redirect the attacker's head. Once inside the attacker's guard, immediately grab the head with both hands and

Salok-saboy first move.

Salok-saboy second move.

and slightly upward twist of the hips towards the *abierta* side of the body.

Methods of Development

The development of *salok-saboy* requires a well-structured approach to ensure that wrist flexibility, strength, timing and accuracy afford the effective and functional application of the technique. A well-balanced methodology will encompass both solo and partner-based training methods to develop the maximum potential of *salok-saboy*.

One solo training method that can greatly enhance the development of *salok-saboy* is to perform the technique in front of a mirror. This is an excellent way to check on the accuracy of the entire fluid motion of *salok-saboy*, especially concerning the alignment of the middle knuckle to lead the strikes and the upward diagonal direction of each strike. When using a mirror to support the development of *salok-saboy*, the technique should be performed deliberately slowly to ensure that accuracy is maintained throughout the entire technique.

Another very useful solo training method is to perform *salok-saboy* using a heavy metal bar to develop strength and flexibility throughout the technique. When using this training method it is essential to maintain structural stability in *salok-saboy* by leading with the middle knuckles of the high hand to establish a correct blade alignment. To develop the appropriate wrist flexibility and strength of delivery, the performance of *salok-saboy* using metal bars should be completed deliberately slowly and without losing the accuracy of form.

Using a training partner to support the

Salok-saboy in front of a mirror.

Salok-saboy using the metal bars.

Salok-saboy against magababayo.

Salok-saboy using focus pads.

development of the *salok-saboy* technique can greatly enhance the timing, accuracy and functionality of performance. The first method to be considered is to perform *salok-saboy* against the training partner attacking with *magababayo* (downward X). This training method uses the right stick against the right stick and the left stick against the left stick and is an excellent way to develop timing, angular alignment, structural stability, blocking and pre-emptive strategies.

A second partner-based training method that can be used to develop timing and accuracy of *salok-saboy* in a dynamic context is to have the training partner use focus mitts. In this training method, the training partner randomly presents the mitts in a pad down position to facilitate the development of timing, accuracy and functional mobility when executing *salok-saboy* under pressure. It is important to ensure that the structural stability and integrity of *salok-saboy* are maintained throughout the technique while developing the skills to apply it against a moving target.

Translation to Other Weapon Categories

Salok-saboy is a key fundamental technique that is fast and fluid in delivery and can be translated easily to other weapon groups. The first translation of *salok-saboy* is to perform the technique using the *tungkod* (staff) in a middle grip with both palms facing down. The first strike uses the right end of the *tungkod* in a diagonally upward direction and travelling from a low right *abierta* position towards a high right *serrada* position. The second strike uses the left end of the *tungkod*, also travelling in a diagonally upward motion from a low left *abierta* position towards a high left *serrada* position. Both strikes should be performed leading with the middle knuckles aligned in a blade orientation to afford structural stability throughout the technique.

Another translation of *salok-saboy* is to execute the technique using a sword. Starting from a right guard with the sword in the right hand, the first motion is a diagonally upward right to left cut, which travels from a low right *abierta* position towards a high right *serrada* position in a circular fashion. The second cut is made in a direction from a low right *serrada* position towards a high right abierta position and is performed in a fluid circulation manner. Both cuts should lead with the cutting edge of the sword to maintain

Salok-saboy using short staff.

structural alignment and accuracy of delivery.

Translation to Empty-Hand Applications

With a strong element of creativity and depth of understanding, *salok-saboy* can be applied effectively to a range of empty-hand situations. Focusing on the angles of attack present in the *salok-saboy* technique, the first translation is applied at medium to close range. Assuming a right lead and having slipped inside the opponent's guard, execute a fast and explosive right uppercut punch that travels from a low right abierta position in a diagonally upward trajectory

Salok-saboy — using the sword.

Salok-saboy inside the opponent's guard.

towards a high right serrada position. The second motion is a right rising back elbow to the face, chest or armpit and this travels from a low right *serrada* origin towards a high right abierta conclusion.

A second option to translate *salok-saboy* into the empty-hand category is to use the motion to apply a locking technique at close range against a right shovel punch to the mid-section. Starting from a left lead stance, as the opponent executes a right shovel punch, withdraw the stomach to evade the punch while simultaneously jamming and deflecting the attack with the right forearm. Pass the left hand over the punching arm and continue diagonally upwards under the attacker's right armpit and grab the right

Salok-saboy against a shovel punch.

GRANDMASTER ANTONIO 'TATANG' ILUSTRISIMO – THE INSPIRATION

Grandmaster Antonio 'Tatang' Ilustrisimo was widely regarded as one of the most skilled, feared and respected Filipino Warriors of all time. While the indigenous martial arts of the Philippines can be traced through several generations of the Ilustrisimo family, it is the unique life experiences and skills of Grandmaster Antonio Ilustrisimo that elevated Kali Ilustrisimo to the revered status that it enjoys today. Not interested in status or financial gain, the lifelong focus of Grandmaster Ilustrisimo was purely about survival and it was not until 1976 at the age of seventy-two years that Tatang eventually accepted his first students, Grandmaster Antonio 'Tony' Diego and Grandmaster Epifanio 'Yuli' Romo. The most senior and respected students of the late Grandmaster Antonio Ilustrisimo, known as the *'Five Pillars of Kali Ilustrisimo'* are:

- The late Grandmaster Antonio 'Tony' Diego of the *Kalis Ilustrisimo Orihinal Repeticion* group and successor to Grandmaster Ilustrisimo
- Grandmaster Epifanio 'Yuli' Romo of the *Bahad Zu'Bu* system
- The late Grandmaster Christopher 'Topher' Ricketts, Chief Instructor of Bakbakan International and the *Kali Ilustrisimo* system
- Grandmaster Reynaldo S. Galang, current Chief

Instructor of *Bakbakan* International and the *Bakbakan Kali Ilustrisimo* system
- The late Punong Guro Edgar Sulite, founder and Chief Instructor of the *Lameco Eskrima* system

Grandmaster Antonio 'Tatang' Ilustrisimo. (Photo: Christopher Ricketts)

shoulder. The second move travels from a low left serrada position towards a high left *abierta* position. This motion is accompanied simultaneously by a right grab and roll of the attacker's right triceps muscle to assist and complete the hammer lock position.

Baguhan – Novice – 'C-shape'

Baguhan is an essential foundation technique from the double weapon methods and is probably one of the most versatile in application. The name *baguhan* means novice, which conveys the simplicity of the C-shaped motion, typical of the type of movement performed by a beginner to the Filipino martial arts. *Baguhan* is a very fluid, twin-striking method that develops the ability to change offensive tactics quickly from high to low targets and from a defensive block or parry to an immediate counter-strike. This very effective fundamental technique develops further into

the intermediate and explosive technique of *bulalakaw* (comet).

Structure and Mechanics

Using the same weapon, *baguhan* consists of two horizontal parallel strikes at different heights. Beginning in the *abierta* (open) position, the first strike of *baguhan* travels horizontally at head height to the *serrada* (closed) side. The second strike starts from the *serrada* position and moves towards the *abierta* side in a horizontal motion at knee height. In structure, the first strike leads with the second knuckles in a blade orientation and with the palm facing vertically upwards. The second strike similarly uses the blade orientation of leading with the second knuckles and has the palm facing vertically downwards. If commencing *baguhan* with the right stick, power is generated in the first strike by twisting the hips sharply to the left. Similarly, the second strike

Baguhan first move.

Baguhan second move.

uses a hip twist to the right to create power in the low backhand strike.

Methods of Development

The *baguhan* technique is capable of generating considerable speed and power during execution and this can be developed by making use of both solo and partner-based supportive training methods. An effective solo training method of developing speed and impact power in executing *baguhan* is to strike a large diameter rope. The first strike is performed palm up and strikes the rope at head height, making full use of body mechanics to generate impact power. The motion travels horizontally from a high *abierta* origin to a high *serrada* finish. The second palm down strike travels from a low serrada position towards a low

abierta completion, also making full use of body mechanics to create impact power. Both strikes should lead with the middle knuckles to ensure that the stability of the technique is maintained.

The development of strength in performing *baguhan* is an essential attribute that can be enhanced through the use of a heavy metal bar for solo training. Starting from a right lead and striking with the metal bar in the right hand, the first movement is a palm up horizontal strike at head height. The strike travels from *abierta* to *serrada* and should be performed intentionally slowly to develop strength at every stage of the motion.

The second move is a low backhand horizontal strike at knee height, travelling from low *serrada* towards low *abierta*. The strike should be executed extremely slowly to ensure the development of the correct form in a strong motion.

Partner-based training can be used to greatly enhance the development and performance of the *baguhan* technique. The first method that can be used to develop speed, accuracy, timing and power of delivery is to perform *baguhan* against a partner using the same technique. In this method the right stick will strike the partner's right stick and the left stick will strike the partner's left stick. Training can be enriched with the addition of random height changes, footwork adaptations and direction adjustments to maximize the benefits of this method.

Another partner-based training method to develop *baguhan* is to have the partner use focus mitts in a dynamic and very mobile environment. Remaining guarded with the two sticks, the partner will flash high and low mitts randomly for the immediate execution of *baguhan*. This method is excellent in developing reaction speed, timing,

Baguhan against the large diameter rope.

Baguhan using the metal bars.

Baguhan striking with the same stick.

Baguhan against the focus pads.

mobility, accuracy and fluidity of motion when performing *baguhan*.

Translation to Other Weapon Categories

Baguhan is a very fast and versatile technique that can be translated freely into other weapon categories. One very effective and powerful translation is to use the *tungkod* (staff) in an end grip. If performing *baguhan* from the right side of the body, the *tungkod* is held at one end with the right hand palm up and the left hand palm down. Driven by a powerful hip twist to the left, the first strike is a horizontal motion at head height and leading with the middle knuckles of the right hand. This powerful first strike travels from right *abierta* to right serrada before flowing in a semi-circle to start the second strike. The second movement is a low backhand right *serrada* to right *abierta* strike aimed at the knee. Power is generated with a sharp right hip twist and the strike continues to lead with the middle right knuckles to ensure structural stability.

Another translation opportunity for using the *tungkod* is in a middle grip with both palms facing down when performing *baguhan*. Starting from the right side of the body, the first strike uses the right end of the *tungkod* in a horizontal motion from right *abierta* towards right *serrada* and leads with the middle right knuckles to ensure blade alignment. The second strike uses the left end of the *tungkod* in a low left *abierta* to left *serrada* trajectory and is aimed at the knee. The second strike leads with the middle left knuckle to ensure that it is structurally sound.

Translation to Empty-Hand Applications

Baguhan is very fast and fluid technique that can be translated easily into empty-hand applications that can include blocking, parrying, striking, trapping, locking or throwing. The first translation can be applied against an attempted left shoulder grab and is applied from a right lead. As the opponent attempts to grab the shoulder with the left hand, use a right *abierta* to *serrada* deflection, moving to the right and to the outside of the attacker's left arm at the same time. The second motion is a right serrada to *abierta* thigh muscle destruction using a hammer-fist smash. This is a very fast and destructive action that can be used as an entry for further techniques or as a defensive strategy

Baguhan using the short staff.

Baguhan using the short staff in a middle grip.

to enable escape.

The second translation of *baguhan* into the empty-hand category allows a rapid switch to the outside position and is applied against a right attempted grab to the left shoulder area. Commencing from a right lead position, as the opponent attempts a right grab of the left shoulder, immediately deflect the attack with the back of the right forearm. The movement travels from right *abierta* towards right serrada and slightly deflects the attempted grab away from the intended target. The second movement is a parry that transfers the attacker's right arm from the high area to the low section and redirects it from low right serrada to low right *abierta* and is accompanied by a switch from right to left stance using exchange footwork. The motion permits zoning to the outside of the attacking arm and is a strong position for a follow-up counter-attack, such as a takedown technique.

Baguhan against a shoulder grab.

Baguhan against an opposite shoulder grab.

CHAPTER 2

INTERMEDIATE TECHNIQUES OF SINAWALI

The development and evolution of effective combative skills is greatly enhanced through progressive and creative training. This chapter continues the journey of exploring the double weapons methods of Filipino martial arts, known collectively as *sinawali*. Building on the fundamental techniques of *sinawali*, a detailed review of the background, structure, development application and translation of some of the many intermediate methods of *sinawali* is provided. The chapter focuses on the intermediate techniques of whirlwind, reverse whirlwind, comet, sun rays and rebounding strikes.

Redonda – Whirlwind

One of the most versatile skills of the double weapon category of Filipino martial arts is the *Redonda* (whirlwind) pattern. The name depicts the ferocity of a high speed circular attack using alternate strikes in a fashion that is as destructive as a whirlwind. Derived from the fundamental *magbabayo* (downward X) sequence, *redonda* uses both weapons in an alternating pattern of rapid and fluid strikes. Descriptive of this rapid action, *redonda* suggests great strength in portraying a whirlwind in motion. *Redonda* can be used both offensively and defensively and, while highly effective in its own right, it informs another intermediate technique, *bukang liwayway* (sun rays) and forms the basis of the more advanced luha redonda (teardrop thrusts with whirlwind) and *pluma bukang liwayway* (pen defence with sun rays).

Structure and Mechanics
Redonda comprises three downward, diagonal circular strikes using alternate weapons during execution. Although the technique can be started from an open stance to disguise intent, it generally commences from a high closed position with both weapons held on the same side and pointing to the rear. If this start is on the right side of the body, then the right stick, which is in the *abierta* (open) position, is held on top at shoulder height and the left stick, which is in the *serrada* (closed) position, is tucked underneath at waist height. The first strike of *redonda* is performed using the top stick and travels inwards and diagonally downwards from shoulder height to hip height in a circular motion that finishes wrapped around the body with the stick held in a *serrada* position and pointing to the rear. The alignment of the hand during the first strike requires the palm to be facing diagonally upwards and the strike leads with the middle knuckles to ensure a blade orientation throughout the motion. The second strike uses the original bottom cane and follows the same diagonally downward line as the first strike. Starting at shoulder height in a *serrada* position, the second strike travels in a backhand motion and diagonally downwards in a circular motion from shoulder height to hip height on the *abierta* side, finishing in the *abierta* position with the stick pointing to the rear. Hand alignment during the second strike is with the palm facing diagonally downwards and, again, this strike leads with the middle knuckle to simulate a blade technique. The third and final strike uses the original top stick, held currently in a *serrada* position. The strike travels in a backhand and diagonally downwards motion from shoulder height towards hip height in a circular trajectory that then returns to the side from which it started to finally tuck underneath the opposite stick and point to the rear. The hand alignment during the third strike is with the palm facing diagonally downwards until it passes the centre line and then turning to palm up, leading with the middle knuckles.

Redonda first move.

Redonda – second move.

Redonda – third move.

Methods of Development

The need to develop strong techniques that can be applied readily and accurately in a wide variety of scenarios is an essential aspect of any martial art training. This section will consider some of the myriad of solo and partner-based training methods that can both enhance the development of the *redonda* technique and provide the opportunity to explore the application of this versatile *sinawali* (double weapon) method. Solo methods of developing redonda include the use of a mirror to develop accuracy, the use of a metal bar to develop wrist strength and the use of a heavy bag to develop impact power. Partner-based training methods to be reviewed include use of the same stick to develop timing, fluidity and blocking skills, using the opposite stick to develop advanced timing

for parrying, and the application of *redonda* against individual single attacks.

Solo training methods used to develop the *redonda* technique commence with practice in front of a mirror. This is an excellent method of checking the alignment of the middle knuckles to simulate blade orientation and for checking the accuracy of executing each strike in a downward, diagonal and circular motion. Mirror training should be performed deliberately slowly to ensure that each stage of *redonda* is accurate and correctly aligned.

Another solo training method that develops *redonda* effectively is the use of metal bars. It is important that the movements with the bars are executed slowly to ensure the development of strength throughout the entire path of each of the

Redonda facing a mirror.

Redonda using the metal bars.

three strikes of *redonda*. This training method is excellent for developing wrist strength and speed of execution when followed by the performance of *redonda* using light sticks. The final solo training method to be considered is the use of the heavy bag to develop impact power. Once range and accuracy of striking the bag are achieved then the *redonda* technique can be performed at full speed and power.

Partner-based training methods are an important and integral aspect of developing the *redonda* technique to a standard where it can be applied readily in a variety of combat situations. The first partner-based training method to develop an effective *redonda* technique is both partners using the same sticks. In this method partners hit right stick against right stick, left stick against left stick and then

right stick against right stick when both partners are starting from the chamber on the right side. This is an excellent training method for developing fluidity of performance, understanding the timing of the technique, becoming accustomed to the feel of impact when striking and for developing a fast *redonda* technique.

The second partner-based training method to be considered is the application of the double stick *redonda* technique against a variety of individual attacks. In this method, one partner serves to feed random strikes at the defending partner, who in turn uses the *redonda* technique to develop skills in application. This method is excellent for developing range, selecting options, flow under pressure and the timing to either block or parry the initial attack.

Redonda striking against the same stick.

Redonda against random single attacks.

Translation to Other Weapon Categories

As a technique, *redonda* in highly versatile and can be applied readily across a wide range of weapon categories. Although the core technique is within the *sinawali* (double weapon) grouping, *redonda* can be applied to single one-handed weapons, single double-handed weapons, flexible weapons and other double weapon classifications. The first option for exploration is to perform the *redonda* pattern using the *tungkod* (staff) held in a central grip. If starting from the right side of the body, a mixed grip is used with the right hand in a palm up grip and the left hand in a palm down grip. First, the right hand end of the staff strikes from *abierta* to *serrada* at head height. The second strike uses the left hand end of the staff to strike from left *serrada* to *abierta* at head height. The final strike uses the right hand end of the staff in a backhand *serrada* to *abierta* motion at head level.

A further translation is to apply the *redonda* pattern using the double weapon *espada y daga* (sword and dagger) category. Assuming a mix of right sword and left dagger and starting from the right side of the body, the first strike would use the sword in a cutting or parrying motion in an inward, diagonally down direction from shoulder height on the *abierta*

Redonda using the short staff in a middle grip.

Redonda using the sword and dagger.

simple defence against an attempted lapel grab, which will develop the timing to respond before the actual grab attack is executed. Assuming that the attacker makes a right handed grab attempt, the first move is to deflect his or her arm with a right *abierta* to *serrada*, across the body open handed, checking motion at a point near the attacking wrist and on the inside of the arm. The second motion is a left handed grab that passes underneath the defending right check, moving from left *serrada* to *abierta* to grab the attacking forearm. The final movement of this empty-hand *redonda* translation is to perform a right backhanded knife-hand strike to the neck or temple area of the opponent in a motion that travels from right *serrada* towards right *abierta*. As the final strike is performed, the left arm simultaneously pulls the

Redonda against a lapel grab.

side to hip height on the serrada side. The second movement could use the knife to execute a *saksak hatak* (palm up thrust with palm down draw cut) at chest height or perform a blade parry from the high *serrada* position to a low abierta finish. Finally, the sword could be used in a backhand cutting or parrying motion from the high *serrada* location in a circular fashion to finish in a low serrada guard.

Translation to Empty-Hand Applications

The speed and versatility of a well-developed *redonda* technique can be translated freely to empty-hand defensive and offensive methods. The technique can be used to block, parry, deflect, grab, trap, lock or strike in a wide range of scenarios. The first empty-hand translation of *redonda* to be considered is a

Redonda against a left lapel grab.

attacking arm forwards to throw the attacker off balance.

A second empty-hand translation option is to perform the *redonda* pattern against an attempted lapel grab with the left hand. As the attacker reaches with the left hand to grab the lapel, perform a right *abierta* to *serrada* across the body deflection to the outside edge of the attacking arm and near to the wrist. The second part of the translation is to perform a left-handed grab by passing the left hand underneath the right check to grasp the attacking wrist in a motion from left *serrada* to left *abierta*. The grab is also an opportunity to slightly knock the attacker off balance with a forward pulling action. The final motion is to execute a right backhanded smash with the forearm to the attacker's left triceps region in a right *serrada* to right *abierta* direction. Finally, roll the attacker's wrist with the left hand while using forearm pressure against the upper arm to perform a straight arm bar.

Redonda Salok-Saboy – Reverse Whirlwind

Also within the same family of *sinawali* (double weapon) methods as *redonda* (whirlwind), *redonda salok-saboy* (reverse whirlwind) is performed in the reverse motion of the parent redonda. As with the *redonda* pattern, the name suggests a highly destructive force that is produced by the rapid upward circular motion of *redonda salok-saboy*. The technique and name are derived from the fundamental technique *salok-saboy* (upward X) and *redonda salok-saboy* also provides fluidity and speed of motion. Often applied in a defensive mode, *redonda salok-saboy* can counter the actions of a *redonda* attack. The reverse whirlwind informs the intermediate *de cuerdas* (rebounding strikes) technique, as well as providing foundation actions for the more advanced *luha redonda* (teardrop thrusts with whirlwind) and *luha salisi* (criss-cross thrusts).

Structure and Mechanics

Redonda salok-saboy includes three upward, diagonal circular strikes that use alternate weapons during the performance of the technique. While it is possible to commence *redonda salok-saboy* from an open stance

to hide the intended strategy, it generally starts from a low parallel position with both weapons held on the same side and pointing to the rear. With a start from the right side of the body, the right stick is held in the *abierta* (open) position at hip height and the tip of the stick is pointing to the rear. The left stick is held in the *serrada* (closed) position above the right stick and is also pointing to the rear. The first strike of *redonda salok-saboy* is performed using the bottom stick held in the *abierta* position. The strike travels inwards and diagonally upwards in a circular motion from hip height on the *abierta* side to shoulder height on the *serrada* side of the body, ending with the stick wrapped around the body and pointing to the rear. Hand alignment during the first strike is with the palm facing diagonally upwards towards the *abierta* side and the technique leads with the middle knuckles in a blade cutting action. The second strike is performed using the original top stick, which travels along the same line as the first strike and starts from hip height in the *serrada* position and strikes diagonally upwards in a circular motion through shoulder height to end pointing to the rear on the *abierta* side. The alignment of the hand during the second strike is with the palm of the hand facing diagonally downwards and the technique leads with the middle knuckles to simulate a blade action. The third and final strike uses the original bottom stick, which is now in the *serrada* position. The strike travels diagonally upwards in a circular motion that travels from hip height on the *serrada* side towards shoulder height on the *abierta* side before returning to finish above the opposite stick in a high *serrada* chamber with the tip of the stick pointing towards the rear. During the third motion of *redonda salok-saboy*, the hand is aligned with the palm facing diagonally downwards and with the technique leading with the middle knuckles.

Methods of Development

The development of *redonda salok-saboy* requires considerable attention to detail because of the wrist alignment required to achieve accurately a blade-oriented technique that can be applied readily and powerfully. This section will consider some individual and partner-based training methods that can be used to support the development of *redonda salok-saboy*. Solo training of *redonda salok-saboy* can make use of a

Redonda salok-saboy first move.

Redonda salok-saboy second move.

Redonda salok-saboy third move.

mirror for accuracy of technique, the use of large diameter sticks to develop wrist and grip strength or heavy rope striking to develop impact power. The partner-based training methods that can support the development of *redonda salok-saboy* include the use of the same stick to develop flow and timing, applying *redonda salok-saboy* against *redonda* to develop a deeper understanding of countering methods and the use of *redonda salok-saboy* against individual strikes to enhance timing and accuracy.

The development of the correct structure and alignment when executing *redonda salok-saboy* is an essential attribute and should be the focus of much solo training. The first focus is to develop great accuracy and this is best achieved by performing the motions slowly in front of a mirror. It is important to monitor and correct the alignment of the middle knuckles during the execution of *redonda salok-saboy*, especially during the first strike where the wrist position may feel a little unnatural at first.

The second solo training method to be applied to the development of *redonda salok-saboy* is the use of large diameter sticks. This training method cannot only

Redonda salok-saboy facing a mirror.

Redonda salok-saboy against the large diameter stick.

Redonda salok-saboy – partner training striking with the same stick.

Redonda salok-saboy against the redonda pattern.

help to improve wrist flexibility gradually but also develop grip strength, which is an essential attribute in all weapons and empty-hand techniques.

The *redonda salok-saboy* technique can be difficult to apply effectively in a combative scenario without many hours of focused partner-based training during the developmental stage. The first training method in developing *redonda salok-saboy* is where both partners strike with the same stick. Starting from the right side of the body, this would be right stick against right stick, left stick against left stick and finally right stick against right stick. This method helps to develop flow, timing, angular alignment and speed of delivery when using the *redonda salok-saboy* technique.

The second method of partner-based training is to use *redonda salok-saboy* against the *redonda* technique, applying upward strikes effectively against downward strikes. This method enhances the understanding of alignment and timing greatly when applying *redonda salok-saboy* in a defensive, combative scenario.

Translation to Other Weapon Categories

Redonda salok-saboy is a technique that requires considerable training to develop but is adaptable freely across the spectrum of weapon categories.

Redonda salok-saboy using the sword and dagger.

Redonda salok-saboy using a single stick.

One option for translation to other weapons is to use the *espada y daga* (sword and dagger) grouping. With a right sword and left dagger mix, the sword executes an upward diagonal cut from the right hip to the left shoulder in a circular *abierta* to *serrada* motion. This movement can be used to cut, block, feint or parry in preparation for the application of the dagger, which performs a straight palm down *saksak* (thrust) at chest level and then retracts to a chamber by the left hip. The final movement uses the sword to perform a backhand upward diagonal cut from the *serrada* hip towards the *abierta* shoulder.

A second option with which to translate *redonda salok-saboy* to another category is to use *solo baston* (single stick). This action can be performed very much in a combative mode and applied with speed and aggression. Assuming a right weapon position, the first move is to strike upwards in a diagonal motion from the right hip to the left to strike or counter-strike in a fluid *abierta* to *serrada* motion. The second motion could be a grab to the opponent's left wrist and pulling him or her forwards and off balance in preparation for the final counter-strike. The final movement is to perform a *serrada* to *abierta* upward diagonal strike using the *punio* (butt of the stick), which travels over the left arm towards the chest or face of the attacker.

Translation to Empty-Hand Applications

As with the *redonda* (whirlwind) pattern, *redonda salok-saboy* provides scope for a diverse range of translations to the empty-hand category. The technique is particularly flexible in offering opportunities to scoop, parry, deflect, lock, strike or

Redonda salok-saboy as a close range punching combination.

Redonda salok-saboy against a mid-section knife attack.

attack the opponent. One option for the translation of *redonda salok-saboy* occurs at a fairly close range. Starting from a left guard position, the first movement of the empty-hand translation is a left hook punch to the temple. This movement leads effectively to the chamber position to start *redonda salok-saboy*. The hook punch is followed immediately by a right uppercut punch to the mid-section of the opponent, travelling underneath the left arm, which is still in the left *serrada* position. The third movement is a hair grab with the left hand that pulls the opponent off balance in a direction towards the left *abierta* side. This drag creates an opening for the final movement of the translation, which is a left back elbow to the floating ribs on the left side of the opponent's body. This latter counter-strike is performed underneath the left arm in a direction from right *serrada* towards right *abierta*.

Another option to translate *redonda salok-saboy* into an empty-hand application is to apply the technique against a right mid-section knife thrust. Starting in a left open hand guard position, the first movement is to use a left scooping action to deflect the incoming attack from left *abierta* towards the left *serrada* side of the body. This motion is used to deflect the attack off-centre and is accompanied by a sharp body twist towards the right side to evade the incoming knife thrust. Once past centre, the second movement is to grab the attacking wrist immediately with the right hand in a position over the top of the attacker's arm. The grab is also used to pull the attacker forwards in the direction of the attack and setting up for the third motion, which is a right back-handed hammer fist strike to the right floating ribs of the attacker. A final very sharp twist to the right enables an arm break or elbow hyper-extension using the left upper arm or left shoulder.

Bulalakaw – Comet

Another technique from the *redonda* (whirlwind) category is the *bulalakaw* (comet), which is derived from the fundamental methods of *salok-saboy* (upward X) and *baguhan* (novice or C shape), as well as the intermediate technique *redonda salok-saboy* (reverse whirlwind). The name suggests a rapid motion, such as can be seen when a comet shoots across the sky at night. *Bulalakaw* is a very fluid technique, which offers opportunities for effective defensive and attacking strategies.

Structure and Mechanics

The *bulalakaw* technique contains three alternate strikes that are executed at different heights, with the first two at head height and the third at waist or leg height. As with all *sinawali* techniques, while it is possible to commence *bulalakaw* from an open position to disguise the intent of the technique, a more general start is from a high parallel position. If the technique is started from the right side of the body, then the right stick is held at shoulder height in the *abierta* position, with the tip of the stick pointing to the rear. The left stick, which is held in a high *serrada* position, is situated above the right stick, also with the tip of the stick pointing to the rear. The first strike of

Bulalakaw first move.

Bulalakaw second move.

Bulalakaw third move.

bulalakaw uses the bottom stick, which is held in the high *abierta* chamber. The strike makes an inward, almost horizontal, motion and has a point of impact at head height. The palm of the hand should be facing upwards and the strike is performed leading with the middle knuckles of the hand to simulate a blade cut. The second strike is made with the original top stick that is currently chambered at shoulder height in the *serrada* position. The second strike is performed in a backhand motion with the palm facing downwards and leading with the middle knuckles, and is aimed at the same head height target as the first strike. As the second strike is executed, the first strike retracts to waist height on the *serrada* side, finishing as the second strike reaches its target. The third and final strike uses the original first stick, which is now chambered at waist height in the *serrada* position. The strike is a backhanded hack to the waist or leg and is performed with the palm facing downwards and the

stick leading with the middle knuckles in a position that simulates the cutting edge of a blade. As the third strike is executed, the opposite stick is retracted above the head with the tip still pointing forwards. This final position of *bulalakaw* is known as *tayong mandirigma*, or warrior stance.

Methods of Development

Bulalakaw is a technique that requires the development of speed and timing to apply it rapidly as a range of combative scenarios. This technique involves the use of wrist strength and flexibility as well as the development of fast and fluid execution. Solo methods can be used to develop the necessary attributes to perform and apply *bulalakaw* rapidly include the use of large diameter sticks to develop wrist strength and flexibility, using metal bars to develop dynamic muscle strength throughout the technique and the use of light sticks on the heavy bag

Bulalakaw using the metal bars.

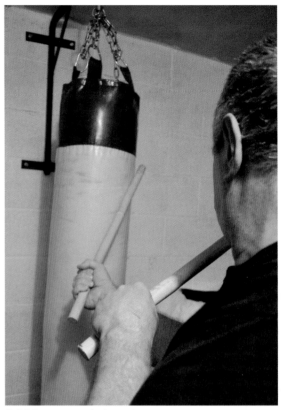

Bulalakaw against the heavy bag.

for speed and impact power development. Partner-based training methods that support the development of timing and agility in the application of *bulalakaw* can include the use of a staff feed to help develop power and timing against strong attacks, using two and three count versions to develop blocking and parrying skills against single attacks and using the same side weapon to develop timing and accuracy during flow.

Solo training methods to support the development of an effective *bulalakaw* technique that can be applied at speed and with fluidity requires some analysis and careful design for maximum benefit. The first method of solo training is to use metal bars, with the *bulalakaw* technique performed slowly to help develop strength throughout the entire range of motion for each strike. When the use of metal bars is followed immediately

with light stick training then considerable increase in speed of delivery should be attained.

The second solo training method to develop speed and impact power is to strike the heavy bag at full speed and with maximum impact. This training method will also help to develop accuracy and range sensitivity when executing bulalakaw with combat speed and power.

The *bulalakaw* technique is fast and very adaptable and can be developed through the use of structured and focused partner-based training. The first training method is to use a partner feeding attacks with a staff. The attacks will need to be high level and either forehand or backhand, which enables the defending partner to apply *bulalakaw* against powerful attacks but also slightly out of range to permit the safe application at full speed and without the risk of injury to the feeding partner.

The second partner-based training method is to apply either the two-count or three-count version of *bulalakaw* against single high level attacks. The two-count version uses one stick to parry the attack while striking the attacking arm simultaneously with the other stick before finishing the technique with a low to middle line final strike. The simultaneous parry and strike method is known as a *gunting* (destruction) method. The three-count version uses a block or parry, with a check to monitor the attack before the final low-line counter-strike.

Translation to Other Weapon Categories

Bulalakaw is a technique that is devastating in both defensive and offensive modes and can be applied readily to other weapons categories within the Filipino martial arts. The first option for translation under review is to perform *bulalakaw* using the *tungkod* (staff). With this weapon, a two-handed central grip is assumed with both palms facing down and the technique will start from the right side of the body. The first two strikes are in rapid succession and use the right hand end of the tungkod to strike twice at the head in a horizontal trajectory from the right *abierta* side towards the right *serrada* side. The third strike uses the left hand end of the *tungkod* to strike from left *abierta* towards left *serrada* at knee height in a horizontal plane.

Another very flexible adaptation of *bulalakaw* from the *sinawali* (double stick) category is to apply the

Bulalakaw against high level staff attacks.

Bulalakaw against a high single strike.

Bulalakaw using the short staff.

Bulalakaw using a single stick.

Translation to Empty-Hand Applications

Bulalakaw is a technique that provides a wide range of flexible options for translation to empty-hand applications. *Bulalakaw* can be used to block, parry, deflect, redirect or strike in a very fluid and aggressive motion. The move is fast and very explosive in execution, and can be applied readily on the inside or outside of an attack. One possible translation of *bulalakaw* can be its application against a high right knife thrust. As the attacker thrusts the knife at chest

Bulalakaw against a high knife thrust.

technique using *solo baston* (single stick). This provides a highly versatile and somewhat aggressive translation option and is effective in a wide range of scenarios. Assuming a right-hand grip with the stick pointing up on the *abierta* side, the first motion is a high level horizontal strike from the *abierta* side of the body towards the *serrada* side. The second motion is performed with the non-weapon alive hand and travels from left *serrada* towards left *abierta* to check, parry or grab the opponent. The second motion travels above the stick in the same horizontal plane. The third strike is a backhand motion at a level between the waist and the knee and moves from right *serrada* through to right *abierta*. With the versatility of single stick *bulalakaw*, it is well worth the investment of time to explore the range of striking, blocking, parrying or feinting options available.

Bulalakaw against a lapel grab.

GRANDMASTER ANTONIO 'TONY' DIEGO – GUARDIAN OF THE LEGACY

Grandmaster Antonio 'Tony' Diego was the designated heir to the system of the late Grandmaster Antonio 'Tatang' Ilustrisimo. Prior to meeting and eventually learning from Grandmaster Ilustrismo in the early 1970s, Grandmaster Diego already had a solid grounding in the Filipino Martial Arts having studied *Balintawak Eskrima* and Modern *Arnis* in the Manila area of the Philippines. Dedicated to preserving the techniques, concepts and strategies learned from Grandmaster Ilustrisimo, it is to his credit that Grandmaster Diego worked tirelessly to

Grandmasters Antonio Diego and Reynaldo S. Galang. (Photo: Reynaldo S. Galang)

Grandmaster Antonio Diego sharing the art. (Photo: Peachie Baron Saguin)

preserve and propagate the devastating methods of *Kalis Ilustrisimo*. Having learned from Tatang in a somewhat unstructured manner, Grandmaster Tony set about providing a structure to the system that would enable the Art to be more readily accessible and understandable to followers of the system. The outcome of a lifetime of dedication is the *Kalis Ilustrisimo Orihinal Repeticion*, which strives to retain and maintain the purity of the original *Kali Ilustrisimo* system. The world of Filipino Martial Arts is poorer after the passing of Grandmaster Tony Diego in August 2014, but the legacy of this great warrior continues in the capable hands of his protégé and successor to the *Kalis Ilustrisimo Orihinal Repeticion* system, Grandmaster Tommy Dy Tang.

height, the first defensive move is to deflect across the body from a right lead position, using the back of the right hand or forearm on the inside of the attack in a right *abierta* to right *serrada* motion. The back of the right arm is used as a safety measure to avoid fatal injuries to the arteries of the inner arm. The second and third moves are almost simultaneous in execution. The second movement is to grab the wrist of the attacking arm with the left hand reaching over the deflecting right arm. The left hand travels from left *serrada* to left *abierta*, grabbing the wrist with the palm of the hand facing outwards. The third move ends fractionally after the left-handed grab and is a right hammer-fist smash to the right side floating ribs of the attacker. The movement is from right *serrada* towards right *abierta* and can continue readily to the right *abierta* side to complete the defence with a right inward elbow to the face of the attacker.

A further translation of double stick *bulalakaw* to the empty-hand category is to apply the movement against a right lapel grab. As soon as the attacker has grabbed the lapel, the first motion is to slap or strike his or her face as a defensive distraction. This initial reactive movement needs to be very fast and explosive to shock and knock the attacker off balance, and the motion continues over the attacker's right grabbing arm. The direction of the first move is from right *abierta* to right *serrada*. The second and third movements are executed simultaneously. The right arm continues in a C-shaped trajectory moving from right *serrada* to a low right *abierta* position, which bends the attacker's arm and forces him or her into an unbalanced posture. As the right arm flows in a C-shape, the left hand is used to tip the head of the attacker backwards in a motion from left *serrada* towards left *abierta*. The simultaneous right and left actions cause the attacker to be weakened considerably and off balance.

Bukang Liwayway – Sun Rays

Informed by the fundamental *magababayo* (downward X) and the intermediate *redonda* (whirlwind) techniques, *bukang liwayway* (sun rays) is a very fast and versatile two-strike combination within the *sinawali* (double weapon) category. The name *bukang liwayway* is given to the technique because the hands are at the centre with the weapon tracing simultaneous opposing rays during the execution of the motion. *Bukang liwayway* provides excellent strategies as a stand alone technique, such as feinting, parrying or striking. Equally, the technique can be applied very effectively in combination with other

techniques, such as *bukang liwaway redonda salok saboy* (sun rays with reverse whirlwind) or *bukang liwayway langit at lupa sinalakot* (sun rays with heaven and earth with vortex). *Bugang liwaway* opens a rapid strategic opportunity to switch tactics from *redonda to redonda salok-saboy* with very little warning of the change.

Structure and Mechanics

Bukang liwayway consists of two alternate strikes that are performed in rapid succession and are aimed at high and low targets respectively. The technique is performed best from an open stance that not only hides the intended motion but also provides scope for alternative strategies to be applied. *Bukang liwayway* is often executed most effectively from a defensive or reverse stance, where the powerful first

Bukang liwayway first move.

Bukang liwayway second move.

rear hand high strike can be applied as a devastating counter-attack. Starting from the open position, the first move is to strike, parry or feint downwards with the front stick, which finishes on the *serrada* side and is tucked underneath the opposite arm, while simultaneously striking powerfully at head height with the rear stick from the *abierta* position. To maintain an appropriate blade orientation when using the stick, the strike is aligned to lead with the middle knuckle, simulating the cutting edge of the sword. At the start of the first strike, there is a slight sidestep to the *abierta* side of the front stick to align the body off centre as part of an evasive strategy. The second strike is achieved by reversing the motion immediately, which involves retracting the first strike over the same shoulder on the *abierta* side while striking simultaneously forwards at a low-line target with the opposite stick from the *serrada* position. As with the first strike, the second strike is performed leading with the middle knuckles to maintain blade alignment. *Bukang liwayway* is similar to and informed by the first strike of the *redonda* (whirlwind) pattern.

Methods of Development

Bukang liwayway is a technique that is deceptively simple and yet requires the development of speed, timing, accuracy and power to enable its effective execution in a combat situation. Using solo training methods, speed of execution can be developed by using metal bars followed by light sticks, impact power can be developed by striking the large diameter rope and accuracy can be enhanced by using a mirror to check the alignment of the technique. Partner training can be used to develop timing and accuracy of *bukang liwayway* in a mobile scenario. This can include same-stick training to develop range and timing, low level attacks to develop parrying skills and the use of focus mitts to develop accuracy of execution against a moving target.

Solo training methods to support the development of an effective *bukang liwayway* technique that can be applied readily in combative scenarios will need to focus on speed, impact power and accuracy of delivery. The first solo training method to be considered is the use of metal bars followed by light rattan sticks to develop speed as well as strength of execution of the *bukang liwayway*

technique. Using the metal bars, the technique should be performed slowly to ensure correct alignment and for the development of strength at all stages of each strike. With an immediate switch to light sticks, *bukang liwayway* should then be performed at full speed and with explosive power.

The second solo training method is to enhance the development of impact power by striking a large diameter rope, which enables a degree of accuracy as well as allowing full force strikes to evolve. Striking the rope will help the development of range appreciation and should be performed at full speed and power.

Partner-based training methods can be used to develop effectively *bukang liwayway*, which is a fast, explosive and versatile technique of the *sinawali* (double weapons) category. The first method of

Bukang liwayway using metal bars.

Bukang liwayway against the heavy rope.

partner-based training is for both partners to strike using the same stick. In this instance and starting from a left stance with *bukang liwayway* starting from the right side of the body, the first high strike would be with both partners using the right stick and the second low strike with both partners using the left stick. This training method can support the development of range appreciation and timing of delivery, and is best practised as a mobile format.

The second training method is for one partner to feed with single, low-line attacks. The defender seeks to deflect the attacks with the initial simultaneous parry and head strike. Again, this is best worked on in a mobile environment, which can greatly enhance your timing, speed and parrying skills. The final training method using the benefit of a partner is to have one partner present random targets with the focus mitts. The defending partner seeks to strike both high and low targets timely using the *bukang liwayway* technique in a mobile and constantly moving setting. This training method can improve greatly the timing, range adjustment, reaction speed and explosive application of *bukang liwayway*.

Bukang liwayway striking with the same stick.

Bukang liwayway against single low-line attacks.

Translation to Other Weapon Categories

Although a two-strike method, *bukang liwayway* is fast and explosive in execution and offers considerable scope beyond the usual double stick option. The first option under review is to translate *bukang liwayway* to the *tungkod* (staff). The technique is to be applied from the right side of the body with the staff in a central double-hand grip, with the right palm facing upwards and the left palm facing downwards. Adopting a left or reverse stance, the first strike is a vertically aligned slightly downward strike at head height using the right end of the *tungkod*. For power and structural stability, the strike leads with the middle knuckles of the right hand for blade alignment. While executing the first strike, the left end of the *tungkod* passes on the right side of the body. Maintaining the vertical alignment of the *tungkod,* the first strike is retracted over the right shoulder while the left end

strikes forwards at groin or thigh height. For structural stability, the second strike leads with the middle knuckles of the left hand. This rapid high to low combination in a vertical plane is both effective and deceptive in application.

Another option for translating *bukang liwayway* is to consider the *espada y daga* (sword and dagger) category. This translation assumes a right sword and left dagger mix and leads from a reverse, or left, stance. Starting from a high open guard position, with the left dagger leading, the first move is performed with the sword. While making a simultaneous low parry with the dagger moving from left *abierta* to left *serrada* in a downward circular motion, the right sword makes a thrust at chest height. The sword motion is from right abierta to a point of impact on the centre line and is performed with the cutting edge of the blade on top and the right palm facing right. As

Bukang liwayway using the short staff.

Bukang liwayway using the sword and dagger.

the sword thrust is retracted to an overhead position, the left knife thrusts from left serrada towards a mid-section centre line target with the left palm facing up.

Translation to Empty-Hand Applications

The *bukang liwayway* technique is fast and explosive and can be translated easily into empty-hand applications. In translation, the technique can be applied readily to block, check, parry, feint, deflect, strike or lock against a diverse range of attacks. One possible empty-hand application can be used against a mid-section knife thrust. The first movement is almost simultaneous and is performed from a left stance with a middle guard. As the attacker executes a right-handed mid-section thrust, step slightly off-line towards the left and perform simultaneously a left-

Bukang liwayway against a mid-section knife thrust.

Bukang liwayway against a lapel grab.

hand deflection with a right hammer-first smash to the attacker's right biceps muscle in a powerful *gunting* (limb destruction) technique. The second move is executed as the right hand grabs and pulls the right triceps muscle while the left forearm redirects the knife hand simultaneously to the rear of the attacker, finishing in a strong hammer lock.

A further empty-hand translation of *bukang liwayway* is an application against a right lapel grab. As soon as the grab is made, make a left palm heel strike at the opponent's face and then divert the left arm over their right grabbing arm, travelling from the left *serrada* side, towards the left *abierta* to return in a circular motion towards the low centre line underneath the attacker's arm. While the left arm is making the circular motion, the right closed fist smashes into the attacker's right clavicle (collarbone), then presses forwards and downwards over the attacker's right shoulder towards the floor. Step behind the attacker with the right leg and execute a tripping throw to take the attacker to the ground and complete the translation technique.

De Cuerdas – Rebounding Strikes

An evolution of the fundamental *salok-saboy* (upward X) and the intermediate *redonda salok-saboy* (reverse whirlwind), *de cuerdas* (rebounding strikes) provides an excellent two-count intermediate technique that works very effectively as a stand alone method. The name indicates the strategic benefit of rebounding from a block into an immediate counter-method. When used alone, *de cuerdas* provides scope for effective feinting, parrying or striking techniques. This technique is excellent when used in combination with other moves, such as *de cuerdas redonda* (rebounding strikes with whirlwind) or *de cuerdas langit at lupa* (rebounding strikes with heaven and earth). As with the reverse motion *bukang liwayway*, *de cuerdas* provides the chance to change direction quickly between *redonda salok-saboy* and *redonda* without indicating the intention of this switch in tactics.

Structure and Mechanics

De cuerdas is made up of two alternating strikes that are performed in quick succession and are aimed respectively at low and high targets. As with the sister move bukang liwayway, this technique is executed most effectively from an open guard position and in a defensive or reversed stance. This strategy supports the selection of the most appropriate technique while benefitting from the power of the rear hand first strike. Starting in a reverse stance, the first strike is performed in a simultaneous action with the front stick completing a hooking parry, feint, or strike upwards and over the serrada (closed) side shoulder. As the front stick retracts, the rear stick circles downwards to the rear on the abierta (open) side before continuing in an upward arc, finishing underneath the opposite stick and sticking upwards towards a low to middle level target, such as the groin or hand. This strike leads with the middle knuckles of the hand to ensure that blade alignment is achieved. This first motion of de cuerdas is influenced and informed by the first strike of redonda salok-saboy (reverse whirlwind). The second strike of de cuerdas is performed by reversing the direction of both sticks simultaneously. The original front stick, which is now in a high serrada chamber above the opposite stick, strikes forwards at head height, leading with the middle knuckle for a strong, blade-based structure. At the same time, the other stick reverses the circular motion to finish in a high chamber on the abierta side, with the stick pointing upwards..

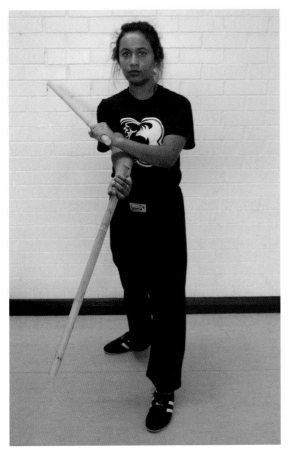

De cuerdas first move.

De cuerdas second move.

Methods of Development

De Cuerdas is a technique that requires the simultaneous use of both sticks in a fast and accurate manner to enable its effective execution in combat. This requires the development of speed, power and accuracy through both solo and partner-based training methods. Solo training can include the use of a fixed stick to develop alignment, using a mirror to develop the accurate execution of *de cuerdas* and using metal bars to develop speed and power. Partner-based training can be used to support the development of agility and timing during the application of *de cuerdas*. This can include single high level attacks to develop timing in parrying and counter-striking, application against *bukang liwayway* (sun rays) to develop timing in blocking and using focus mitts to develop range, timing and accuracy of execution against a non-static target.

Solo training can greatly enhance the development of the *de cuerdas* technique into a highly effective and versatile combative method. With the lack of a training partner there is a need for some creativity in training and the first solo training method to help develop *de cuerdas* is the use of a fixed stick. The fixed stick can be used to simulate either a weapon or an attacking arm and allows for the development of a slight side shift together with a fast parry with simultaneous counter-strike. With the stick or staff fixed pointing slightly upwards, the upper end can be used for the parry with the lower portion as a target for the counter-strike.

The second very useful method of solo training is to use a mirror for regular checks of technique alignment, leading with the middle knuckles for blade awareness enhancement and accuracy of delivery, especially during the first strike. *De cuerdas* is a technique that demands speed and power in delivery and this can be improved greatly by using metal bars as a training tool. The technique should be performed deliberately slowly with the aim of developing strength and each stage of the motion and followed immediately with light stick performance to assess the impact of the metal bars on speed development.

The use of partner-based training methods to develop the fast and flexible *de cuerdas* technique is an essential element of the complete development of this method. The first partner-based training approach is to have the partner feed single, high level attacks so that the attributes of range adjustment, speed and timing are honed to a functional and effective standard. Assuming a left stance, as the partner attacks with a high right-handed inward strike, the left stick is used to parry from *abierta* to *serrada*. In a

De cuerdas against a fixed stick. *De cuerdas facing a mirror.* *De cuerdas against a single high attack.*

De cuerdas against bukang liwayway.

simultaneous motion in the opposite direction, the right stick performs a fast and explosive uppercut motion travelling from *abierta* towards the *serrada* side of the body.

The second training method is to have the attacker feed with the *bukang liwayway* (sun rays) technique. The high strike of *bukang liwayway* can parried with the high stick while the low stick strikes the lower stick of the training partner. This develops excellent timing in using *sima* (hooking parry) and the simultaneous counter-strike of *de cuerdas*. The final training method is for the partner to wear focus mitts and present random pad down targets for an explosive *de cuerdas* strike in a dynamic and mobile context. This training method helps to develop excellent timing, accuracy and power against a moving and random target.

Translation to Other weapon Categories

De cuerdas is a highly effective and deceptive technique that can translate readily into other weapons categories to provide a fast and explosive addition to the repertoire. The first translation is to perform *de cuerdas* using *solo baston* (single stick) against attacks on the high line. Assuming a left lead with the stick in the right hand, the opponent attacks with a right overhead strike towards the head. Use the left alive hand to parry and deflect the attack from

the left *abierta* side towards left *serrada* side of the body. As the parry is made, execute a fast upward diagonal strike with the stick, travelling from right *abierta* towards right *serrada* and finishing at stomach height. The strike leads with the middle knuckles to ensure structural stability and blade orientation.

A second option for translating the *de cuerdas* technique into a different weapon category is to use the *tungkod* (staff). This method provides a very fast and devastating simultaneous parry and counter-strike option when using the *tungkod* in defensive mode. Assume a left lead stance, holding the *tungkod* in a middle grip with the left palm up and the right palm down. As the attacker makes a right overhead strike towards the head, use the left end of the *tungkod* to perform *sima* (hooking parry), which deflects the attack from the high left *abierta* side to the high left *serrada* side of the body. As the parry is made, the right end of the *tungkod* is directed towards the groin of the attacker in an upward circular motion and travelling from right *abierta* towards the centre line.

De cuerdas using a single stick.

De cuerdas using the short staff with a middle grip.

Translation to Empty-Hand Applications

As a technique, *de cuerdas* provides a range of empty-hand translation options for an effective, simultaneous defensive strategy. The empty-hand version of *de cuerdas* can be used effectively to block, strike, destroy or lock the opponent. The first translation is performed from a left guard position and against a right cross punch; in a simultaneous motion, use a left parry to deflect the incoming punch slightly in a motion from the left *abierta* towards the left *serrada* position. At the same time, perform a *gunting* (limb destruction) technique to the attacker's right biceps muscle with a right, middle knuckle punch that travels diagonally upwards from right *abierta* towards right *serrada*.

Another option to translate the *de cuerdas* technique into the empty-hand category is to apply it at close range in a grappling scenario. Slip inside the attacker's guard in a left stance and with a high guard position. Grab the back of the attacker's neck immediately with the left hand and pull him or her forwards and off balance. Simultaneously, execute an explosive right palm up shovel punch to the solar plexus or mid-section of the body. This application makes use of, and is informed by, the hand positioning when performing the double stick version of the *de cuerdas* technique.

De cuerdas against a right cross punch.

De cuerdas in a grappling scenario.

CHAPTER 3

ADVANCED TECHNIQUES OF SINAWALI

All martial arts provide scope for the evolution of the practitioner through consistent and relentless practice, known as *subli*. Through this the ability to execute the most advanced concepts and strategies of the martial arts is realized. This chapter will provide a clear and detailed overview of the advanced techniques of the double weapon category known as *sinawali*. Building on the skills, knowledge and strategies of the fundamental and intermediate *sinawali* methods, the exploration considers the background, structure, development, translation and application of some of the more advanced techniques from the family of twin weapons combat. Specifically, the chapter will explore the techniques of teardrop thrusts with whirlwind, criss-cross thrusts, pen defence with sun rays, double parry with fan strike and double parry with tunnel thrust.

Luha Redonda – Teardrop Thrusts with Whirlwind

One of the more advanced techniques within the *redonda* (whirlwind) family, *luha redonda* (teardrop thrusts with whirlwind) is a fast and explosive sequence of defensive and counter-attacking strategies. The name of the technique reflects the devastating impact of the double thrust techniques that are combined with the destructive power of a whirlwind. *Luha redonda* is derived from the fundamental *magbabayo* (downward X) and *salok-saboy* (upward X), as well as the intermediate *redonda* and *redonda salok-saboy* (reverse whirlwind) techniques.

The technique also incorporates the very effective *tulay* (bridge) and *lagusan* (tunnel) techniques. *Luha redonda* can be used defensively to parry and counter simultaneously and offensively to thrust, interrupt

timing and strike the opponent.

Structure and Mechanics

Luha redonda comprises five movements, which includes a simultaneous parry and low thrust, a checking motion, a high thrust and two diagonal circular strikes. The technique commences from a high open guard position, which disguises the intent of the practitioner and allows for flexibility in defensive or offensive strategies. Starting from a left stance with a high guard, the first move is to parry with the left stick in a motion from a high left *abierta* (open) position towards a middle level left *serrada* (closed position). As the parry is performed, the right stick makes a slightly upward thrust at stomach height and travels from a low right *abierta* location towards a centre line target. This combination is collectively known as *tulay* (bridge thrust).

The second move is to withdraw the left foot while executing a check with the left stick that travels from left *serrada* towards left *abierta* with the stick pointing towards the right side of the body. The third motion involves a forward step with the right foot while delivering a high right thrust over the left stick towards the chest of the opponent. The thrust travels from a high right *abierta* position towards the centre line at chest height and concludes by continuing towards right *serrada*, where it finishes fully closed. The fourth technique is a left, diagonally downward, circular strike that travels from a high left *serrada* origin towards a low left *abierta* conclusion, leading with the middle knuckles at all times to maintain structural stability. The final move of *luha redonda* is a right backhand strike that travels from a high right *serrada* position towards a point of impact of the centre line. The trajectory is a downward, diagonal, circular left to right motion. This technique also leads

Luha redonda first move.

Luha redonda second move.

Luha redonda third move.

Luha redonda fourth move.

Luha redonda fifth move.

with the middle knuckles to ensure blade alignment and the stability of the strike.

Methods of Development

As with the fundamental and intermediate techniques in the *sinawali* (double weapon) category, the advanced technique of *luha redonda* requires a highly structured approach to allow the development of maximum potential. The use of both solo and partner-based training methods can greatly enhance coordination, fluidity, accuracy, timing and power, and both formats are essential for the overall development of this technique. Solo training methods to be reviewed include the use of a mirror to develop accuracy of motion and the use of metal bars to develop strength throughout the technique. Partner-based training methods that can enhance the development of *luha redonda* can include the use of focus pads for the development of accuracy in the thrusting technique of *tulay* (bridge thrust) and *lagusan* (tunnel thrust). Another method is to have the training partner feed high level attacks to improve timing, accuracy of application and range development.

The first solo training method to develop a fast and efficient *luha redonda* is to perform the technique slowly in front of a mirror. The focus should be on developing accuracy of motion and performance that does not waste unnecessary motion. The mirror is excellent for checking the alignment of the weapon, ensuring particularly that the strikes lead with the middle knuckle during the second, fourth and fifth moves.

Another solo training method is to use metal bars when practising *luha redonda*. When using this method it is important to perform each stage of the technique deliberately slowly so that grip and wrist strength are developed fully throughout the entire range of motion for each move of the *luha redonda*. It will be important to ensure correct blade alignment

Luha redonda using focus pads.

Luha redonda facing a mirror.

Luha redonda using metal bars.

Luha redonda against single high level attacks.

by leading with the middle knuckles on the striking motions.

The core attributes of timing, accuracy, speed, explosiveness and range adjustment can all be greatly enhanced during partner-based training activities. The first partner-based training method is to have the partner wear focus pads and present targets for the *tulay* (bridge thrust) and *lagusan* (tunnel thrust) sections of the *luha redonda* technique. This training method should be dynamic with a full mobile training partner presenting random targets for the two thrusting techniques to considerably improve timing, range adjustment and accuracy of the motions.

The second partner-based training method is to have the partner feed with a high level attack, which could be either a forehand or backhand *bagsak* (downward diagonal strike) or *tusok* (thrust). This training method should again be very mobile and dynamic and is used to enhance the timing of the parry into the initial bridge thrust.

Luha redonda using the short staff.

Luha redonda using the sword and dagger combination.

Translation to Other Weapon Categories

The speed, coordination and flexibility of *luha redonda* ensures its relatively easy translation across weapon categories. The first translation is to perform *luha redonda* using the *tungkod* (short staff). Assume a left stance with the *tungkod* held centrally on the right side of the body and with the left palm down and right palm up. The first move is a thrust to the body with the left end of the staff, which is followed immediately by a second thrust at chest height with the right end of the *tungkod*. The left end is then used for a striking technique that travels from a high left *serrada* origin towards a low left *abierta* conclusion. The final motion is a right backhand strike that travels from a high right *serrada* position towards middle right *abierta*, but ending on the centre line.

The second translation is to perform *luha redonda* using *espada y daga* (sword and dagger). Adopt a left lead start with the *espada* (sword) in the right hand normal grip and the *daga* (dagger) in a left hand normal grip. The first move is a high left *abierta* to middle left *serrada* parry with the dagger while delivering a sword thrust to the mid-section. This is followed by a transitional withdrawal of the right foot while checking forwards with the dagger before immediately launching into a chest level sword thrust

that travels from high right *abierta* towards the centre line while you step into a right stance. The fourth move is high left *serrada* to middle left *abierta* slash with the dagger and the sequence finishes with a high right *serrada* to middle centre line slash with the espada. It is essential that all slashing motions are delivered with accuracy by ensuring that they lead with the cutting edge of the blade.

Translation to Empty-Hand Applications

Luha redonda is a fast and explosive method that translates well to creative empty-hand applications. One option makes use of the first three motions of the technique in an aggressive and pressing attacking mode. The first movement, tulay, is a simultaneous left hand head grab and a mid-section shovel punch with the right fist at close range. The grab moves from a high left *abierta* origin towards a middle left *serrada* finish while the right punch travels from low right *abierta* towards a middle centre line conclusion. The second motion is to use the left forearm to push at chest height with the left arm moving from middle left *serrada* and pressing forwards on the centre line. The final *lagusan* movement is a right lunge punch

Luha redonda as a forward pressing attack.

Luha redonda in a grappling scenario.

of a right elbow strike over the left pushing arm and travelling forwards towards the centre line from a high right *abierta* origin.

Luha Salisi – Criss-Cross Thrusts

A technique from within the *redonda* (whirlwind) category, *luha salisi* (criss-cross thrusts) provides the strategic opportunity to switch sides and rapidly counter with devastating thrusting techniques at different levels. The name of this technique describes appropriately the core motion of thrusting towards opposing corners of the body. *Luha salisi* is informed by and derived from the fundamental *salok-saboy* (upward X) and *magbabayo* (downward X), and includes influences from the intermediate *redonda* and *redonda salok-saboy* (reverse whirlwind). The technique is also influenced by the advanced *luha redonda* (teardrop thrusts with whirlwind) sequence. As with the sister technique of *luha redonda*, this move also includes the devastating *tulay* (bridge) and *lagusan* (tunnel) methods of parrying and thrusting simultaneously.

Structure and Mechanics

The technique *luha salisi* consists of four movements and includes a low thrust, two parries and a high thrust. *Luha salisi* begins from an open position, which provides the strategic advantage of flexibility of action as well as preserving the element of surprise when using this very effective technique. Beginning from a left stance with a high guard, the first move is to parry with the left stick in a motion from a high left *abierta* (open) position towards a middle level left *serrada* (closed position). At the same time as the parry is implemented, the right stick makes a slightly upward thrust at stomach height and travels from a low right *abierta* location towards a centre line target. The second movement uses the left stick to execute a high vertical parry that progresses from the low left *serrada* position towards a high left *abierta* conclusion, at the same time as the left foot is retracted adjacent to the right foot. The third movement begins by stepping forwards with the right foot and completing simultaneously a high right vertical parry that travels

delivered over the left pressing forearm and is aimed at the face area, travelling from high right *abierta* towards a high centre line ending.

Another possible translation to empty hands is applied at close range and makes use of the first three moves of *luha redonda*. In this case, the tulay consists of a head grab with the left hand travelling from a high left *abierta* origin and pulling towards the middle height centre line finish, with a simultaneous right fingertip pressing choke with the right palm facing up and moving from high right *abierta* towards the centre line. The second action is a left unbalancing face push in a motion from a high left *serrada* start and pressing forwards on centre. This creates an opening for delivering the finishing *lagusan* in the form

Luha salisi first move.

Luha salisi second move.

Luha salisi third move.

Luha salisi fourth move.

from a high right *abierta* origin towards a high right *serrada* finish. Finally, and while remaining in the right stance, the left cane completes a chest level thrust over the top of the right arm that travels from a high left *abierta* location towards the centre line. The combination of the parry and high chest thrust is known as *lagusan* (tunnel thrust).

Methods of Development

Luha salisi is a technique that requires considerable developmental training to execute effectively the opposite side thrusts that are performed at different heights. The need for power, accuracy, timing and wrist strength are essential attributes that can be enhanced effectively through solo and partner-based training methods. Solo training can include using a heavy bag to develop impact power when executing the thrust techniques and an understanding of the adaptability of parrying motions into striking techniques. Another effective solo training method is to use metal bars to develop wrist and grip strength throughout the technique. The dynamic and very mobile partner training methods of using focus pads or having the partner feed random attacks can greatly enhance the timing, accuracy and range adjustment.

A very effective solo training method of developing *luha salisi* is to use a heavy bag. This is especially useful in gauging wrist and grip strength on impact on the two thrusting techniques and the method can further enhance overall performance when the two parries are delivered as fast and powerful strikes between the two thrusts. When replacing the parry techniques with a strike, it is important to lead with the middle knuckles to ensure structural stability and blade alignment.

A second solo method of developing a strong and fluid *luha salisi* technique is to use metal bars during performance. This method should be done slowly and can improve greatly grip and wrist strength, both of which are essential for a fast, powerful and accurate technique.

The development of effective timing, range adjustment and explosive power when executing *luha salisi* can best be achieved through partner-based training. The first method is to have the partner wear focus pads and present random targets for the *tulay*

Luha salisi against the heavy bag.

Luha salisi using metal bars.

Luha salisi using focus pads.

Luha salisi against random high level attacks.

timing, accuracy and the necessary range adjustment to apply *luha salisi* effectively against a constantly moving and unpredictable target.

Translation to Other Weapon Categories

Luha salisi is a fast and explosive technique that readily supports the translation across weapon groupings. The first translation is to execute luha salisi using *solo baston* (single stick). Commencing in a right stance with the stick held in the right hand and in a high abierta guard, the first move is a right *sima* (hooking parry) or *sungkite* (hooking thrust), which travels from a high right *abierta* origin towards a conclusion at a middle right *serrada* position. The second motion is a *palis* (parry) with the stick travelling from middle right *serrada* towards a high right *abierta* conclusion. Switching to a left stance, the third move is a check or parry with the left alive hand, travelling from a high left *abierta* origin to a middle left *serrada* conclusion. The final movement is a *lagusan* (tunnel thrust) with the stick travelling from a high right *abierta* start and finishing on centre line.

The second translation is to perform *luha salisi* using *espada y daga* (sword and dagger). Begin in a right lead with the sword in a right normal grip and

(bridge thrust) and *lagusan* (tunnel thrust) components of *luha salisi*. This method can greatly enhance timing, accuracy and range adjustment when performed in a very mobile and dynamic environment.

The second method of partner-based training is to have the attacker feed random high level strikes or thrusts from either the abierta position or from the *serrada* position. This training method will improve

Luha salisi using single stick.

Luha salisi using the sword and dagger.

the dagger in a left normal grip. The first move is a right *sima* (hooking parry) travelling from a high right *abierta* position to middle right *serrada* position while simultaneously executing a left middle section dagger thrust. The next move is a middle right *serrada* towards high right *abierta* slash with the dagger while changing to a left stance. The third motion is a slash with the dagger that moves from a high left *abierta* origin to conclude in a middle left *serrada* position. The technique concludes by thrusting the sword over the top of the dagger towards the centre line from a high right *abierta* origin.

Translation to Empty-Hand Applications

Luha salishi is a fast and effective method that translates well into the empty-hand category. The first application makes use of the second, third and fourth movements of the combination and begins in a right stance with a low unassuming guard. Against a right grab attempt, the first move is a middle right parry that travels from a middle right *serrada* position and concludes at a middle right *abierta* point. Stepping forwards to a left stance, the second motion is to check the elbow of the attacking arm with a left parry travelling from middle left *abierta* towards the centre line. Finally, the counter is *lagusan*, which is a high right punch that originates at a high right *abierta* position and concludes at a high centre line point.

A second application of *luha salisi* makes use of the second and third moves to apply a locking technique against a right push attempt. Assume a right stance with a low unassuming guard and parry the incoming right arm at the wrist in a motion from middle right *serrada* to middle right *abierta*. The movement ends in a wrist grab while stepping back into a left stance to knock the opponent off balance. The second movement is to apply pressure to the back of the incoming upper arm by using the left forearm in a movement from middle left *abierta* towards low left *serrada*. This movement is accompanied by a clockwise rotation of the attacking wrist with the right hand to complete the arm bar lock.

Luha salisi against a right push.

Luha salisi against a right grab.

GRANDMASTER REYNALDO S. GALANG – THE SCHOLARLY WARRIOR

Grandmaster Reynaldo S. Galang is the current head of Bakbakan International and has long been a key driving force in sharing and spreading the Filipino Martial Arts on the international arena. One of the 'Five Pillars' of *Kali Ilustrisimo*, Grandmaster Rey is educated, articulate and highly logical in his approach structuring a refined and accessible training methodology. Grandmaster Rey developed the *Bakbakan Kali Ilustrisimo* system, also known simply as *Bakbakan Kali* and he also provided considerable input and structure to the *Lameco Eskrima* system of the late Punong Guro Edgar Sulite. It is this logical and highly structured approach that has produced countless champions in the international tournament arena and that has made the

Bakbakan Kali Ilustrisimo system more widely accessible to practitioners regardless of geographic location. Widely respected as a leading exponent of *Sinawali*, the twin weapons aspect of the Filipino Martial Arts, Grandmaster Rey is a well-established historian and author of the indigenous martial arts of the Philippines. Most notably, Grandmaster Rey is generous in his efforts to afford a platform for leading exponents of the Filipino Martial Arts, providing substantial coverage to diverse systems within his ground-breaking books, *Warrior Arts of the Philippines* and *Masters of the Blade*.

Grandmaster Reynaldo S. Galang – a leading authority on sinawali. (Photo: David Foggie)

Grandmaster Reynaldo S. Galang, current head of Bakbakan International. (Photo: David Foggie)

Pluma Bukang Liwayway – Pen Defence with Sun Rays

Pluma bukang liwayway (pen defence with sun rays) is a sub-technique from the *redonda* (whirlwind) family and provides the opportunity for a rapid switch from defensive to offensive strategies. The name of the move hides the devastating effectiveness achieved during execution and is more descriptive of the hands that are at the centre with the weapon tracing simultaneous opposing rays during application. *Pluma bukang liwayway* is derived from and informed mainly by the fundamental *magbabayo* (downward X), the intermediate *redonda* (whirlwind) and *bukang liwayway* (sun rays) techniques. The combination of a high defence and immediate high counter followed by

a low counter can be extremely effective in application.

Structure and Mechanics

Pluma bukang liwayway is made up of three movements and features a high open defence followed immediately by high then low strikes. Allowing for some flexibility in application and disguising the intended action, *pluma bukang liwayway* begins from an open guard position. Assuming a left stance, the first move is a left *sima* (hooking parry), which travels from a high left *abierta* (open) origin towards a middle left *serrada* (closed) conclusion. Simultaneously to the hooking parry, the right fist travels in an uppercut-type motion, leading with the *punio* (butt of the stick) and on the inside of the left parry to conclude in a high position with the tip of the

Pluma bukang liwayway first move.

Pluma bukang liwayway second move.

Pluma bukang liwayway third move.

stick pointing downwards. Collectively the left parry and right stick motion are known as *pluma* (pen defence). These motions with the sticks are accompanied by a very slight left sidestep to move off the line of attack while executing the defence. The second move is a strike to head height with the rear stick from the *abierta* (open) position. To maintain an appropriate blade orientation when using the stick, the strike is aligned to lead with the middle knuckle, simulating the cutting edge of the sword. The third strike is completed by reversing the motion immediately, which involves retracting the second strike over the same shoulder on the *abierta* side while striking simultaneously forwards at a low-line target with the opposite stick from the *serrada* position. As with the second strike, the second is performed leading with the middle knuckles to maintain blade alignment.

Methods of Development

As an advanced technique from the *sinawali* (double weapon) category, *pluma bukang liwayway* requires considerable dedicated training to develop the speed, timing, accuracy and coordination to execute this effective defensive and counter-offensive combination technique. Solo training methods can greatly enhance the accuracy and coordination requirements of the technique and can include the use of a mirror for accuracy and using metal bars to develop strength and coordination.

Solo training methods can help develop the accuracy and coordination required to perform *pluma bukang liwayway* under the pressure of a combative scenario. The first and very useful method of developing accuracy is to perform the technique in front of a mirror. This method should be performed slowly and precisely, ensuring that the small sidestep is accompanied by the simultaneous *sima* and *pluma* before counter-striking with the *bukang liwayway* (sun rays) strikes.

The second solo training method is to perform *pluma bukang liwayway* using metal bars. This training

Pluma bukang liwayway facing a mirror.

Pluma bukang liwayway using metal bars.

Pluma bukang liwayway against single high level attacks.

Pluma bukang liwayway against stick and focus pad.

method forces the slow and deliberate execution of the technique while developing combative strength throughout the entire motion. A further enhancement can be to use normal sticks after the performance with metal bars to develop speed and explosiveness while maintaining accuracy of movement.

To develop the required timing, range adjustment and speed to perform *pluma bukang liwayway*, a range of partner-based training options are available. The first to be considered is to have the partner attack with single high level strikes or thrusts from either an *abierta* or *serrada* origin. This method should be performed in a mobile and random fashion to create opportunities to develop combative attributes under pressure.

Another partner-based training method to support the development of *pluma bukang liwayway* is to have the partner use a single stick to feed with high level attacks while wearing a focus pad to present a target for the *bukang liwayway* high level counter-strike. This method not only develops the timing to defend in a dynamic and constantly moving environment, but also allows for the development of a powerful and accurate initial counter-strike.

Translation to Other Weapon Categories

Pluma bukang liwayway is a fast and destructive defensive method that translates freely across weapon categories. The first translation is to perform the technique using *solo baston* (single stick), commencing in a left stance and with the stick held in a right normal grip and assuming a low right *abierta* guard. Perform a simultaneous high left *abierta* toward middle left *serrada* parry while simultaneously executing a right *pluma* by driving the *punio* (butt) of the stick upward and inside the left parrying arm. The *pluma* travels from a low right *abierta* origin towards a high right *serrada* conclusion. The second motion is to immediately strike forwards with the stick towards the head in a trajectory from high right *abierta* towards the centre line. Finally, the left hand is used in a pushing motion, travelling from middle left *serrada* towards the centre line at chest height.

The second translation is to perform *pluma bukang liwayway* using a *tungkod* (short staff). Assume a left stance with the tungkod held at one end with the

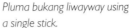

Pluma bukang liwayway using a single stick.

Pluma bukang liwayway using the short staff.

right hand over the left hand and left palm down with right palm up. The staff is held in a low right chamber and the first move is to perform *pluma* driving the butt end of the staff upwards from a low right *abierta* beginning to a high right serrada conclusion and with the tip of the stick pointing downwards. This move is accompanied with a slight left sidestep to move off the centre line. The second move is to strike at head height, with the tip of the stick travelling forwards from a low right *abierta* origin to a conclusion on the centre line. This motion is then reversed in a clockwise circle, travelling from a high centre line position to circle on the right *abierta* side of the body and concluding on the centre line at groin height. To ensure structural stability, the middle knuckles should lead in all striking actions with the *tungkod*.

Translation to Empty-Hand Applications

Pluma bukang liwayway is a method that translates readily into close range empty-hand applications. One option for translation is to apply the technique within a clinch position with the first motion being a right rising elbow strike to the chin. The elbow travels from a low right *abierta* position towards a high centre line conclusion and could be adapted easily to an

Pluma bukang liwayway against a swinging punch.

Pluma bukang liwayway against a clinch attack.

uppercut punch as the situation dictates. The action could be accompanied with a left head grab that travels in a pulling motion from left *abierta* towards the centre line. The second rapid follow-up action is to deliver a fast hammer-fist strike to the face with the right fist travelling forwards along the centre line from the high centre line origin created by the rising elbow technique.

Another application is to apply *pluma bukang liwayway* as an entry to a throwing technique that is applied against a swinging punch attempt. From a right stance with a middle guard, drive the right palm heel upwards and into the shoulder to jolt the opponent, while simultaneously maintaining cover with the left hand in a high left abierta guard. The palm heel strike travels from a low right *abierta* origin towards a high right *serrada* conclusion. Trapping the attacking right arm by wrapping the left arm around it in an anti-clockwise rotation, shift forwards to hook the right leg behind the attacker's right leg and apply a downward diagonal pressure to the shoulder with the right palm heel to execute a tripping throw.

Palis Nakaw Abaniko – Double Parry with Inside Fan Strike

A sub-method from the *redonda* (whirlwind) grouping, *palis nakaw abaniko* (double parry with inside fan strike) is a rapid combination that enables very fast and effective defensive manoeuvres to be executed. This technique provides a solid defensive strategy from the *serrada* (closed) position and the name is very descriptive of two parrying techniques followed by a fan strike. *Palis palis nakaw abaniko* is derived from the fundamental *salok-saboy* (upward X) and the intermediate *redonda salok-saboy* (reverse whirlwind) techniques. This technique is also influenced by the advanced *luha salisi* (criss-cross thrusts) method. The rapid flow and flexibility of *palis nakaw abaniko* make it a very effective and explosive combination of moves, with the potential for application in a range of diverse scenarios.

Structure and Mechanics

Palis palis nakaw abaniko comprises three movements that embrace a *serrada* (closed) to *abierta* (open) parry, an *abierta* to *serrada* parry and a high inside fan strike. Commencing from a right, open, guarded position, which provides the element of surprise in disguising the intended tactics, *palis palis nakaw abaniko* is deceptively fast and fluid in the execution of defence and counter-attack methods. The first move is a high right *serrada* to high right *abierta* parry with the stick vertically aligned as the right foot is withdrawn adjacent to the left foot. An adjustment of alignment could transpose this parry easily into an effective pre-emptive striking method. The second motion requires a step forward with the left foot while executing a

Palis palis nakaw abaniko first move.

Palis palis nakaw abaniko second move.

Palis palis nakaw abaniko third move.

high left parry with a vertically positioned stick. This parry travels from high left *serrada* to high left *abierta* and could also be adjusted to provide a striking opportunity. The final technique of *palis palis nakaw abaniko* is to perform a right inside fan strike over the left parrying arm. The right *abaniko* (fan strike) is aimed at the right side of the opponent's head or neck and travels in a circular arc on a horizontal plane, moving from high right *abierta* to high right *serrada*, then back towards high right *abierta*. The fan strike is executed largely with a wrist rotation and a slight extension of the right arm towards the opponent.

Methods of Development

As with the sister technique of *luha salisi* (criss-cross thrusts), *palis palis nakaw abaniko* requires the development of fast and accurate parries to create the opportunity for the inside fan strike counter-attack. The required attributes can be developed readily through the solo training methods of rope striking or using a mirror to improve accuracy. Enhanced timing and the development of creative defensive methods can be considerably improved during partner-based training, which can either be

random single or double attacks, or using a staff to facilitate the development of destructive power during each movement.

The first solo training method is to perform *palis palis nakaw abaniko* against a large diameter rope. This training method enables an understanding that the *palis* (parry) techniques can be interchanged freely to become very fast, powerful and effective striking methods. The rope enables the strikes to be performed at full speed and power, improving range adjustment and without the potential drag that can occur when striking a heavy bag.

The second solo training method is to perform *palis palis nakaw abaniko* in front of a mirror to develop a fast and accurate execution of each component of the technique. Initially the move should be performed deliberately slowly to ensure that accuracy is developed and, once achieved, you should aspire towards a full speed performance while maintaining total accuracy.

The development of the necessary speed, timing, power and accuracy to deliver a destructive *palis palis nakaw abaniko* is best achieved during partner-assisted training. The first training method is to have

Palis palis nakaw abaniko against the large diameter rope.

Palis palis nakaw abaniko facing a mirror.

the partner feed random single or double strikes, leading with either the right or left stick and originating from either an *abierta* or *serrada* position. This training routine should be dynamic, random and very mobile to enhance the development or speed, timing and accuracy when defending against either single or double random attacks.

The second partner-based training method is to have the training partner use a *tungkod* (staff) to present a target randomly for striking with all three components or *palis palis nakaw abaniko*. This training option should be mobile and the staff can be presented at a variety of heights to develop the power and flexibility to perform the technique under

Palis palis nakaw abaniko against random attacks.

Palis palis nakaw abaniko against short staff attacks.

the pressure of a combat situation.

Translation to Other Weapon Categories

A fast, explosive and decisive technique, *palis palis nakaw abaniko* has the flexibility to translate across most weapon categories, providing a very effective defensive strategy. The first translation is to perform the technique using the *tungkod* (short staff) from a right stance, holding the staff in a central grip with the right palm up and the left palm down and with the staff held vertically on the left side of the body and the right hand uppermost. The first move is a high right *serrada* to high right abierta motion to execute a high section *palis* (parry). The second motion is to lower the right hand end and perform a high left *abierta* to high left *serrada* parry with the left end of the cane pointing upwards. Finally, the *abaniko* (fan strike) is performed with the right end of the *tungkod* travelling anti-clockwise from high right *abierta* to conclude at high right *serrada* and with the left end of the *tungkod* tucked under the right armpit in a high left *serrada* position.

The second translation is to perform *palis palis nakaw abaniko* using the *solo baston* (single stick).

Commencing in a right stance with the stick held in a right normal grip and held in a middle right *serrada* guard position, the first move is a middle right *serrada* (closed to high right *abierta palis* (parry) performed with the stick pointing upwards. The second movement is to perform a left check which travels from high left *abierta* to middle left *serrada* and with the palm of the left open hand leading. The last movement is to perform the *nakaw abaniko* (inside fan strike) by looping the stick around the head in an anti-clockwise motion starting from high right *abierta* and finishing in a high right *serrada* position.

Translation to Empty-Hand Applications

Palis palis nakaw abaniko is a fast and explosive technique that translates freely into empty-hand applications. The first translation is to use the three

Palis palis nakaw abaniko smashing through a strong guard.

Palis palis nakaw abaniko using the short staff.

Palis palis nakaw abaniko using a single stick.

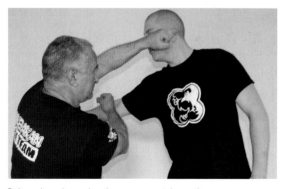

Palis palis nakaw abaniko against a right push.

motions to smash through the guard to deliver a final neck strike. Driving forwards in a right stance, the first movement is to parry the opponent's guard using the right hand in a motion that travels from a middle right *serrada* location towards a middle right *abierta* conclusion. The second parry with the left hand is used to reinforce the redirection of the guard by pushing in a direction towards middle left *serrada* from a middle left abierta start position. The second movement seeks to trap the guard of the opponent and create an opportunity for a final knife-hand strike to neck with the right hand travelling from a high right *abierta* origin towards a high centre line conclusion.

Another translation to the empty-hand category is to use *palis palis nakaw abaniko* as an entry to a throwing technique. Against a right push attempt, the first movement is to deflect the incoming arm using a right parry that travels from a middle right *serrada* beginning towards a middle right *abierta* end. The second action is to engage with the parried right arm using a left parry that progresses from a middle left

abierta origin through middle left *serrada* and circling clockwise towards a low left *abierta* concluding with a grab of the wrist with the left hand. Deliver a right knife-hand strike to the neck of the opponent in an action from high right *serrada* towards the centre line. At this point, grab the neck and circle both hands clockwise in a motion that raises the attacker's right arm with the left hand while the head is moved to a hip height position to complete the axil throw.

Palis Palis Lagusan – Double Parry with Tunnel Thrust

Another sub-technique from the *redonda* (whirlwind) family is *palis palis lagusan* (double parry with tunnel thrust). This technique is a speedy combination that allows the practitioner to perform very explosive defensive strategies. As with the sister technique of *palis palis nakaw abaniko* (double parry with inside fan strike), *palis palis lagusan* provides a very useful

Palis palis lagusan first move.

Palis palis lagusan second move.

Palis palis lagusan third move.

strategy to defend from the *serrada* (closed) chamber position. The technique is informed by the fundamental *salok-saboy* (upward X) and the intermediate *redonda salok-saboy* (reverse whirlwind) and *redonda* methods, with further influences from the advanced *luha salisi* (criss-cross thrusts technique. The speed of execution makes this a very flexible method that can be adapted comfortably to both defensive and offensive strategies.

Structure and Mechanics

The technique *palis palis lagusan* is made up of three fluid movements and includes a high *serrada* (closed) to high *abierta* (open) parry, a high *abierta* to high *serrada* parry and a final high level tunnel thrust. Affording a wide range of defensive options, *palis palis lagusan* starts from an open guarded position. Assuming a right open stance position, the first move of *palis palis lagusan* is to perform a high right *serrada* to high right *abierta* parry with the stick aligned vertically. As the first parry is executed, the right foot is retracted next to the left foot in preparation for the second movement. Stepping forwards with the left foot, execute a high left *abierta* to high left *serrada* parry with the stick in vertical alignment. While described as *palis* (parrying) motions, both the first and second motions can be adjusted easily into highly effective striking methods. The concluding movement of *palis palis lagusan* is the execution of a right tunnel thrust over the left parrying arm. The tunnel thrust commences from a high right *abierta* position and travels forwards towards a centre line target at chest or face level with the right palm facing down.

Methods of Development

Palis palis lagusan requires a similar development strategy to the sister technique of *palis palis nakaw abaniko* (double parry with inside fan strike) but with the need for accuracy in the *lagusan* (tunnel thrust) motion that is found in *luha salisi* (criss-cross thrusts). Solo training methods to support the development of a fast, accurate and powerful execution of the technique can include using a mirror to enhance the accuracy of performance. Using metal bars is another solo training method that can support the enhancement of power throughout the delivery of *palis palis lagusan*. The evolution of combative

Palis palis lagusan facing a mirror.

Palis palis lagusan using metal bars.

attributes is best supported during partner-based training and can include the use of a focus pad and stick to develop timing and accuracy and the feeding of random high level attacks to improve timing and range adjustment.

The first solo training method to support the development of *palis palis lagusan* is to perform the technique slowly while facing a mirror. The training method can be used to check on the accuracy of the two parrying movements and the finishing thrust, as well as the switching of stance during performance.

The second training method is to use metal bars during execution to develop combative power during each component of *palis palis lagusan*. The nature of this training method ensures a slow and accurate performance of the technique while developing grip

Palis palis lagusan against the stick and focus pad.

Palis palis lagusan against random attacks.

and wrist strength and overall power of performance.

The development of combat ready skills and attributes requires the use of partner-supported training to maximize the performance of *palis palis lagusan*. The first training method is to have the partner wear a focus pad on one hand and attack with single high level strikes or thrusts with a stick. This training option should be very mobile and the attacks should be performed at random and with the simultaneous presentation of the focus pad as a target for the *lagusan* (tunnel thrust). The goal should be to effectively parry and check the attack and deliver a thrust to the centre of the focus pad.

A further partner-based training method is to have the partner feed with random high level attacks with either the right or left stick and from a *serrada* or *abierta* origin. As with any partner drills, this method should be very mobile, fast and random so that maximum skills are developed to parry, check and counter the attack. Options to use the second parry as a striking motion should be explored according to the range of available targets that are open during the activity.

Translation to Other Weapon Categories

As with the sister technique of *palis palis nakaw abaniko* (double parry with inside fan strike), speed, explosiveness and destructive power are core to the effective translation of *palis palis lagusan* to other weapon categories. The first translation is to perform the move using *espada y daga* (sword and dagger) with the *espada* (sword) held in a right normal grip and the *daga* (dagger) held in a left normal grip. Commence in a left stance with the sword held in a middle *serrada* position and the dagger held below the sword in a middle left *abierta* guard. The first move is a sword parry travelling from middle right *serrada* to high right *abierta* and with the sword pointing upwards. The second movement is a left slash from the middle left *abierta* origin to a high left *serrada* conclusion. Finally, perform *tusok* (thrust) with the sword travelling from high right *abierta* above the left dagger and towards a high centre line conclusion.

The second translation is to execute *palis palis lagusan* using the *tungkod* (short staff). Start from a left stance with the staff held in a central grip on the left side of the body and with the right palm up and

Palis palis lagusan using the sword and dagger.

Palis palis lagusan using the short staff.

the left palm down. The first move is a high right *serrada* to high right *abierta* motion to execute a high section palis (parry). The second motion is to lower the right hand end and perform a high left *abierta* to high left *serrada* parry with the left end of the cane pointing upwards. The third motion is to use the left end of the *tungkod* to deliver a *tusok* (thrust) from high left *serrada* towards a high centre line target.

Translation to Empty-Hand Applications

Palis palis lagusan is a fast and flexible technique that transfers well in the empty-hand category. The first application using the technique deflects and zones around the opponent's attack before a finishing counter-strike. Starting in a right stance, the first movement deflects the opponent's guard using a right parrying action that travels from a middle right *serrada* origin towards a middle right *abierta*

conclusion and is accompanied by stepping diagonally forwards to a left stance. The second motion is a left shoulder grab that moves from the left *abierta* position and pulls towards the centre line. Finally, deliver the *lagusan* (tunnel thrust) in the form of a right palm heel strike to the side of the head that travels from a middle right *abierta* position to end in a high centre line position.

A further application is to apply *palis palis lagusan* inside the opponent's guard and while moving from middle to close range. Pressing forwards and inside the guard, the first move is to redirect the opponent's outstretched left arm by using a right *palis* (parry) that moves from the centre line towards a middle right *abierta* conclusion. Continuing the forward pressing action, the second move is a left head grab that travels from a high left *abierta* origin to grab the back of the head and pull it forwards along the centre line. The final finishing action is to deliver a powerful high right forearm smash that progresses from a high right *abierta* start and travels explosively forwards along the centre line to contact with the face of the opponent.

Palis palis lagusan against an aggressive guard.

Palis palis lagusan moving to close range.

SOLO BASTON

The use of the *solo baston* (single stick) as a training implement and a weapon is a very common practice in the Filipino martial arts and this widespread use highlights the importance of this category in the repertoire of the exponent. Through the practice of techniques in this category, the practitioner gains a sophisticated appreciation of *anggulo* (likely angles of attack), *tiyempo* (timing), *pagkilos* (mobility) and the refined use of the *bantay-kamay* (guardian hand) to control, trap and manipulate the opponent. This component is a dominant feature of stick-fighting tournaments because of the great speed and fluidity of motion that make it challenging for exponents, as well as being very exciting for spectators. Techniques within the *solo baston* category translate freely to other single weapon groups, such as the *tungkod* (staff), *kalis* (sword) or *baraw* (knife) but are less adaptable to the flexible weapons grouping. The placement of a weapon in the *bantay-kamay* further affords translation into the twin weapons category of

Bagsak using single stick.

Bagsak using the short staff.

Bagsak using empty hands.

sinawali by using either *doble baston* (double sticks) or *espada y daga* (sword and dagger).

This section of the book provides a detailed exploration of some of the fundamental, intermediate and advanced techniques contained within the *solo baston* category. Each technique is investigated with the establishment of a technical overview and the identification of opportunities to develop the movements through solo or partner-based training methodologies. The scope to translate techniques to other weapon categories is explored and options for empty-hand adaptations are identified and analyzed.

CHAPTER 4

FUNDAMENTAL TECHNIQUES OF SOLO BASTON

A strong foundation in any martial practice is essential for the development, understanding and application of strong combat-effective skills. This chapter will offer a detailed review of the most fundamental methods of the single stick category of the Filipino martial arts known as *solo baston*. Consideration is provided in relation to the background, structure, development through solo and partner-based training, translation and application of these basic combative methods. The chapter will investigate the techniques of downward diagonal strike with thrust, horizontal and vertical strikes, low to high rebounding strikes, star block with upward diagonal strike and twin fan strikes.

Bagsak Salok – Downward Diagonal Strike with Thrust

Perhaps the most basic motion when using *solo baston* (single stick) is *bagsak salok* (downward diagonal strike with thrust). This technique has various forms of delivery and can be performed with a vertical or diagonal alignment. The current review and analysis will consider the diagonal version of the *bagsak salok* technique. The name is derived from two words with *bagsak* referring to a downward smashing action and *salok* meaning to scoop, which reflects the action of the upward thrust portion of the *bagsak salok* technique. The diagonal version of *bagsak salok* is informed by and is part of the basic *sinawali* (double weapon) technique of *magbabayo* (downward X) technique. *Bagsak salok* can inform and develop the intermediate techniques of *de cuerdas arriba bagsak* (high to low rebounding strikes with downward strike) and *sima bagsak* (hooking parry with downward strike). The technique further evolves into the advanced methods of *sima bagsak salungat*

(hooking parry with opposite side downward strike), *Estrella boklis abaniko bagsak* (star defence with upward strike, fan strike and downward strike) and *bulalakaw bagsak* (comet with downward strike).

Structure and Mechanics

The *solo baston* technique of *bagsak salok* consists of two techniques that travel on the same diagonal line and in opposite directions. *Bagsak salok* commences from a right stance with the stick held in the right hand and in a high chamber. The first motion *bagsak* (downward strike) starts from a high right *abierta* (open) position and travels to a low right *serrada* (closed) position at waist height. As the first strike is performed, the right foot steps back into a left stance while the hips twist towards the left to gain maximum power in the strike. At the conclusion of the *bagsak*

Bagsak salok first move.   *Bagsak salok second move.*

technique, the tip of the stick remains pointing forward towards the opponent and throughout the motion the strike leads with the middle knuckles for blade orientation. The second movement commences with a simultaneous step forward with the right foot as the stick thrusts diagonally upwards from the low right *serrada* origin towards the high right *abierta* conclusion. This second movement travels along the same line as the first *bagsak* technique but in the opposite direction and leads with the tip of the stick.

Methods of Development

The first solo training method to be reviewed is to perform *bagsak salok* in front of a mirror. Using this method, the technique should be performed deliberately slowly to ensure accuracy of delivery, with particular attention being paid to blade alignment by leading with the middle knuckle, not over-striking by

Bagsak salok against the large diameter rope.

keeping the tip of the stick pointing towards the imaginary opponent and the use of full hip twist to maximize power.

The second solo training method is to strike a large diameter rope using *bagsak salok*. This training method is excellent for developing range adjustment, destructive impact power and increasing wrist and grip strength at the point of impact. Care should be taken to ensure the correct alignment and structural stability by leading with the middle knuckles, which also helps to avoid wrist injuries on impact with the target.

The first partner-supported training method is to have the partner feed single random strikes or thrusts in a dynamic and very mobile setting. The partner should wear a padded glove and the purpose is to develop the accuracy and timing in delivering a powerful hand strike, which is followed immediately by a thrusting motion. It can be useful to experiment by using the *salok* (thrust) as a *sima* (hooking parry) to deflect the attack before countering with a powerful *bagsak* (downward diagonal strike).

The second training method is to have the partner wear focus pads and present random low targets for the *bagsak* strike or a high target for the *salok* thrust.

Bagsak salok facing a mirror.

Bagsak salok using a padded glove.

Bagsak salok using focus pads.

This method should be very mobile and performed in a way so as to enhance reaction speed, as well as accuracy and impact power of both elements of *bagsak salok*.

Translation to Other Weapon Categories

Bagsak salok is a powerful and explosive method that transfers easily to other weapon groups. One translation is to perform the technique using a *tungkod* (staff) held at one end, with the right hand palm up and over the left hand, which is palm down. Begin in a right stance with the *tungkod* held in a high

right *abierta* guard and the first move is *bagsak* (downward diagonal strike), which leads with the middle knuckles for blade alignment. The strike travels from the high right *abierta* origin to a low right *serrada* conclusion and is accompanied by a simultaneous stepping back with the right leg to facilitate power generation. The *salok* (thrust) is performed by stepping forward with the right leg while thrusting diagonally upwards from a low right *serrada* start to end in a high right *abierta* position.

Another translation of *bagsak salok* is to use *espada y daga* (sword and dagger). Using the *espada* (sword) in a right normal grip and the *daga* (dagger) in a left normal grip, assume a right stance with the sword held in a high right *abierta* guard and the dagger held in a low left *abierta* guard. While stepping back with the right leg, the sword cuts from the high right *abierta* position to a low right *serrada* finish. At the same time, the dagger thrusts upwards in a *sima*

Bagsak salok using the short staff.

Bagsak salok using the sword and dagger.

Bagsak salok against a right lapel grab.

Bagsak salok against a right grab.

(hooking parry) motion, travelling from a low left abierta origin to conclude in a high left *serrada* position. The second movement requires stepping forward with the right leg while slashing diagonally downwards from high left *serrada* to a low left *abierta* end. Simultaneously, the sword thrusts diagonally upwards from a low right *serrada* position to a high right *abierta* conclusion.

Translation to Empty-Hand Applications

The fundamental technique of *bagsak salok* translates readily to the empty-hand category. One option is to apply the move as a counter to a right lapel grab. The first movement is to step back with the left foot into a deep left stance while holding the attacker's right hand with the left hand. At the same time, use the right forearm to deliver an arm drag that travels from a high right *serrada* position on top of the opponent's right elbow joint and progresses downwards towards a low right *serrada* conclusion. The second action is to smash the thumb edge of the right forearm into the face of the attacker in a movement from a low right *serrada* origin towards a high right *serrada* conclusion. Finally, grab the head of the opponent and pivot on the right foot while turning the back on the opponent and twisting the hips sharply to the left to execute a neck throw.

The second application is against an attempted right grab and uses the *bagsak* as a limb destruction against the reaching right arm of the opponent. The motion uses the little finger edge of the forearm to deliver the destruction in a motion from high right *abierta* towards a middle right *serrada* finish. Turning the right palm down, reverse the motion to strike into the face with the outer forearm in a motion travelling from a low right *serrada* towards a high right *abierta* conclusion.

Planchada Doblete – Horizontal and Vertical Strikes

Another basic motion of the *solo baston* (single stick) category is *planchada doblete* (horizontal and vertical strikes). The name of the technique is descriptive of the horizontal and vertical downward motions of the stick and the latter vertical movement may be termed as *redonda* or *redondo* (circular vertical strike) in some systems of the Filipino martial arts. *Planchada doblete* is very much a stand alone fundamental method that can develop into the intermediate *tusok alon* (wave thrust) of the *solo baston* classification.

Planchada doblette first move.   Planchada doblette second move.

Structure and Mechanics

Planchada doblete comprises two strikes that are perpendicular to each other, with the first being in a horizontal plane and the second being vertically aligned. Starting from a right stance with the stick held in the right hand and setting a high guard, the first move is *planchada* (horizontal strike. It travels from a right *abierta* (open) origin to right *serrada* (closed) conclusion with the palm facing up until past the target area, where it turns palm down and finishes with the stick pointing to the rear on the *serrada* side at waist height. It is important to lead with the middle knuckles for blade alignment and for the structural stability of the motion. The second move is *doblete* (vertical circular strike), which begins from the middle low *serrada* position with the palm facing down. The strike travels in a clockwise circular motion on the *serrada* side of the body, moving from right *serrada* towards the centre line with the right palm facing left and then returns to the *serrada* position with the palm facing down. The second strike makes a very fast and powerful vertical strike in a complete circle and should lead with the middle knuckles to ensure stability and strength in the movement.

Methods of Development

The development of wrist strength and flexibility can be achieved during solo practice by using the metal bar to replace the stick and performing *planchada doblete* deliberately slowly. While caution should be observed because of the wrist torque during execution, the technique will benefit greatly in terms of grip, wrist and overall strength throughout the entire technique while using the metal bar.

Rope striking is another effective solo training method that can improve range adjustment significantly and have an impact on power during the performance or *planchada doblete*. The focus can either be on the horizontal strike to develop maximum destructive power, then performing a vertical strike beside the rope, or executing the *doblete* strike in a diagonal fashion to allow impact on the rope with both strikes. It is important to maintain correct structure and alignment when striking the rope to avoid wrist injuries.

Training with a partner is the best method of enhancing the core combative attributes of timing,

Planchada doblette using the metal bar.

Planchada doblette against the large diameter rope.

Planchada doblette against stick and focus pad.

mobility and range adjustment. The first training method is to have a partner using a stick and focus pad while feeding single high level attacks during mobile practice. The focus pad can be used to develop power on either the *planchada* (horizontal strike) or *doblete* (vertical strike) against a mobile opponent.

The second training method is to have the partner feed single attacks with the stick, with the focus of developing the necessary timing and range adjustment, including zoning to deliver *planchada doblete* against a moving target in a very dynamic environment. While both partner-based methods should be carried out under the pressure of speed, mobility and aggression, care should be taken to ensure the accuracy and integrity of this very adaptable technique.

Planchada doblette against random attacks.

Translation to Other Weapon Categories

Planchada doblete is a powerful and fluid technique that translates readily to other weapon groupings. The first translation to be considered is to execute *planchada doblete* using *doble baston* (double sticks).

Planchada doblette using double sticks.

Planchada doblette using the short staff.

Begin from a right stance with both sticks held in normal grip and chambered in a middle *abierta* guard. While the right stick performs *planchada* (horizontal strike) travelling from middle right *abierta* to a middle right *serrada* conclusion, the left stick performs a *palis* (parry) travelling above the right stick from middle left *abierta* to middle left *serrada*. Keeping the left stick in the middle *serrada* position, the right stick executes a *doblete* (vertical strike) by circling forwards and downwards on the right *serrada* side of the body. Step back with the right foot simultaneously to generate power in the *doblete* strike.

Another possible translation is to deliver *planchada doblete* using the *tungkod* (short staff) held at one end with the right hand palm up and above the left hand, which is palm down. Commencing from a right stance with the staff in a middle right *abierta* guard, the first strike travels horizontally from middle right *abierta* to a right *serrada* conclusion. The *tungkod* then circles forwards and downwards on the right *serrada* side of the body to complete the *doblete* (vertical strike) technique. The second strike is accompanied by stepping back with the right foot to generate maximum impact power.

Translation to Empty-Hand Applications

Planchada doblete is a technique that can translate well to the empty-hand category of the Filipino martial arts. One possible translation is to apply the move against a right wrist grab using the right hand. As soon as the wrist is grabbed, hold the opponent's right hand with the left hand and take the right hand across the body travelling horizontally from a middle right *abierta* origin to conclude at a middle right *serrada* position. Maintaining the left grip on the opponent's right hand, circle the right hand clockwise on the *serrada* side of the body to finish over the right wrist of the opponent and continue downwards towards the centre line to apply a painful wrist lock effectively.

The second application is against a right shoulder grab and begins with an immediate limb destruction using the middle right knuckles to strike the right biceps muscle. The motion travels from a high right *abierta* position and progresses horizontally towards a high right *serrada* ending. Once contact is made with the opponent's biceps muscle, strike immediately

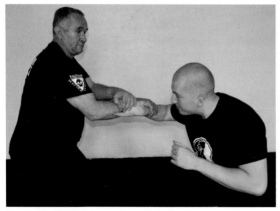

Planchada doblette against a wrist grab.

Planchada doblette against a shoulder grab.

vertically forwards in a clockwise arc along the centre line to finish with a hammer-fist strike to the forehead of the opponent.

De Cuerdas Abajo – Low to High Rebounding Strikes

Perhaps advanced in concept and strategic advantages, another fundamental technique in the *solo baston* (single stick) category is *de cuerdas abajo* (low to high rebounding strikes). The name of this move is descriptive and refers to the action of rebounding from the opponent's blocking technique and countering immediately with another strike using the energy from the rebound action. In the case of *de*

cuerdas abajo, the first strike is low and the rebound strike is at a high target. *De cuerdas abajo* is informed and influenced by the fundamental *sinawali* (double weapon) techniques of *salok-saboy* (upward X) and *magbabayo* (downward X) in terms of the lines of the strikes. There are also influences from the intermediate double stick technique of *de cuerdas* (rebounding strikes). Conceptually and strategically, *de cuerdas abajo* informs the intermediate *solo baston* technique of *de cuerdas arriba bagsak* (high to low rebounding strikes with downward strike).

Structure and Mechanics

De cuerdas abajo is made up of two strikes that are aligned diagonally and travel in opposite directions along the same line. With the stick in the right hand and beginning in a right stance, the first strike commences from a low right *abierta* (open) position and strikes towards *serrada* (closed) in a diagonally upward trajectory stopping before the centre line at waist height. Structurally, the first strike leads with the

De cuerdas abajo first move.

De cuerdas abajo second move.

Methods of Development

De cuerdas abajo requires a high degree of wrist flexibility, accuracy, spatial awareness, timing and power. The first solo training method to support the development of this strategically advantageous

De cuerdas abajo facing a mirror.

middle knuckles to ensure correct blade alignment and strength of movement. While the name suggests a rebound either off the opponent or from a blocking technique, the first motion of *de cuerdas abajo* could also be used as an *enganyo* (feint) to draw the opponent's defence and create a high opening for the successive strike. The second strike occurs as a reversal of the first motion, initially travelling downwards towards a low right *abierta* position and continuing in an anti-clockwise diagonal rotation towards a high right *serrada* target, striking through and returning in a full circle to a low right *abierta* conclusion. The second strike of *de cuerdas abajo* travels diagonally on the same line as the first strike, but in the opposite direction and leads with the middle knuckles of the hand to maintain blade orientation and structural stability.

De cuerdas abajo using the metal bar.

technique is to perform the move while facing a mirror. The technique should initially be performed slowly to ensure that the correct angular and blade alignment is achieved throughout the combination. Structural stability is essential if wrist injuries are to be avoided.

The second solo training method is to use a metal bar when performing *de cuerdas abajo* and this strategy will greatly enhance wrist strength and flexibility to support the development of a very fast and explosive technique. When using the metal bar the technique should be performed deliberately slowly and should be followed by repetition using a standard rattan cane, where speed can be introduced to the execution of the movements.

To develop *de cuerdas abajo* to a level of combat functionality requires the adoption of focused partner-based training methods. The first method is to simply have the partner block or defend against low line *abierta* or *serrada* attacks. The focus of this evolutionary training method is initially to gain an acute awareness of the openings and opportunities created by the defensive actions of the training partner. The timing can either be to rebound from the defensive motion to counter-strike at the opposite corner of the body, or to perform an *enganyo* (feinting technique) to draw the partner's defence and then redirect the motion to strike another part of the body before stick contact is made.

The second training method is to have the partner wear focus pads and present simultaneous low and high targets at random and while in motion. The *de cuerdas abajo* technique should be executed rapidly to develop speed and impact power against a moving opponent.

Translation to Other Weapon Categories

While fundamental in the *solo baston* category, *de cuerdas abajo* is advanced in concept and translates

De cuerdas abajo as a counter to a low block.

De cuerdas abajo against focus pads.

De cuerdas abajo using the sword.

De cuerdas abajo using the short staff.

circle anti-clockwise to strike through a high right serrada target before concluding in a low right *abierta* position.

Translation to Empty-Hand Applications

De cuerdas abajo is a deceptively effective method that translates freely into empty-hand applications. One such application is applied in a close range clinch scenario and the first move is a right palm up shovel punch to the mid-section. This move progresses from a low right *abierta* starting point and travels slightly upwards towards the centre line. Retract the punch and circle it anti-clockwise on the right *abierta* side of the body to grab the opponent's hair at a high centre line point. The move is then finished with a driving right knee to the mid-section of the opponent while

De cuerdas abajo against a clinch attack.

freely to other types of weapons used in the Filipino martial arts. A natural progression is to perform the technique using the *espada* (sword) held in the right hand and commencing in a middle right *abierta* guard position. The first movement is a diagonally upward cut that begins from a low right *abierta* origin and travels towards a middle centre line target. The sword then reverses motion and circles anti-clockwise from the middle centre line origin to cut through a high right *serrada* target and concludes in the low right *abierta* guard.

The second translation of *de cuerdas abajo* is to use the *tungkod* (short staff) to execute the technique. Starting in a right stance with the *tungkod* held at one end, right palm up over left palm down double grip, the guard is a middle right *abierta* position. The first strike travels diagonally upwards from a low *abierta* beginning position towards a middle centre line target and leads with the middle knuckles of both hands for stability of the structure of this powerful technique. The *tungkod* rebounds to

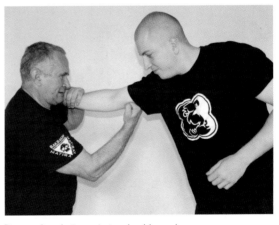

De cuerdas abajo against a shoulder grab.

pulling the head downwards.

Another application of *de cuerdas abajo* is against a right shoulder grab. The first motion is to grab the opponent's right hand with the left hand while simultaneously delivering a right diagonally upward hammer-fist strike to the triceps area which begins at a low right *serrada* point and travels towards a high right serrada conclusion. Circle the right fist clockwise on the *serrada* side to make contact on top of the opponent's right elbow joint, then step backwards into left stance to complete the arm drag to knock the opponent off balance. The arm drag moves from the high right *serrada* contact point towards a low right *serrada* concluding position.

Estrella Boklis – Star block with Upward Diagonal Strike

A very important basic technique within the *solo baston* (single stick) grouping is *estrella boklis* (star block with upward diagonal strike). The name of this basic defence and counter method is descriptive of the star block and subsequent upward diagonal counter. *Estrella boklis* is informed by and derived from the fundamental *sinawali* (double weapon) techniques of *salok-saboy* (upward X) and *baguhan* (C-shape), as well as the intermediate *sinawali* techniques of *redonda salok-saboy* (reverse whirlwind) and *bulalakaw* (comet). This technique informs and evolves into the advanced *solo baston* method of *estrella boklis abaniko bagsak* (star defence with upward strike, fan strike and downward strike).

Structure and Mechanics

Estrella boklis is a basic defence and counter-method that comprises two fluid movements, incorporating a defensive block or parry on the *serrada* (closed side) that immediately continues into an upward diagonal counter from the *serrada* side. Assuming a right stance with the stick held in the right hand in a middle right *abierta* (open) guard, the first move travels across the body from *abierta* to *serrada* with the stick pointing upwards. It concludes with the middle knuckles pointing to the rear and with the left alive hand checking over the top of the right stick hand. Dependent on the origin, the first motion can

Estrella boklis first move.

Estrella boklis second move.

progress in an upward circular fashion, in the same manner as the *sinawali* (double weapon) technique of *salok-saboy* (upward X). The second move flows from the first as the stick circles anti-clockwise towards the rear *serrada* side before travelling downwards then forwards to complete an upward diagonal strike towards the armpit on the right *serrada* side of the body. The second motion travels from the low *serrada* position towards the centre line, but concludes still on the *serrada* side of the body. This counter-strike leads with the middle knuckles to ensure that the correct structure and blade alignment is maintained throughout the technique.

Methods of Development

The development of *estrella boklis* requires accuracy of motion, timing, flexibility, range adjustment, explosive power and excellent coordination. The first solo method of developing this technique is to use a mirror to check every detail of motion. Particular attention should be paid to body shifting, hip twist and the correct blade alignment during performance. The performance of *estrella boklis* should be deliberately

Estrella boklis against the large diameter rope.

slow so that a high degree of accuracy can be achieved.

The second solo training method that can enhance range adjustment and the development of explosive power is to strike a large diameter rope. While the *estrella* (star block) is a defensive action, it could be used as a strike when engaged in rope training, or the blocking function can be maintained by body shifting and by using the correct defensive alignment. This should be followed immediately by the *boklis* (upward diagonal cut) and the combination should be fluid, in range and very explosive in application.

When developing the core attributes of timing, accuracy, range adjustment and coordination, it is appropriate to make use of partner-based training methods. The first activity is to have the training partner feed with high level strikes or thrusts from either the *abierta* position or from the *serrada* origin. This activity should be very mobile and dynamic with the attacks performed at an increasingly faster pace until full speed is achieved. The defender will use the *estrella boklis* to defend against the incoming attacks and will use *estrella serrada* (star block on the closed side) or *estrella abierta* (star block on the open side) as appropriate.

The second partner-based drill is to have the partner use a stick and focus pad, presenting a stick strike for the *estrella* defence and a focus pad target

Estrella boklis facing a mirror.

Estrella boklis against high random attacks.

Estrella boklis against stick and focus pad.

position with the cutting edge of the sword facing the rear to facilitate a flat of the blade blocking motion. As the sword passes the centre line, the left knife can execute *lagusan* (tunnel thrust) over the top of the right arm and this begins in a middle left *abierta* position, travelling palm down towards a centre line target. The second motion of *estrella boklis* is to deliver the *boklis* (upward diagonal strike), progressing from the *estrella* to travel from low right *serrada* towards the middle to high centre line in a diagonal cutting action aimed at the armpit area.

A second translation across the weapon groupings is to perform *estrella boklis* using the *tungkod* (short staff). Commence from a right stance with the *tungkod* held at one end right hand palm up over left hand palm down and with the staff held in a right *abierta* middle level chamber. The first move is *estrella* (star block), which travels from the middle right

Estrella boklis using the sword and dagger.

for the *boklis* counter-strike. This training method should also be very mobile and fast paced to enable the defender to switch from defence to counter-striking in a fast and fluid, explosive manner.

Translation to Other Weapon Categories

Estrella bokis is a fast and powerful technique that lends itself freely to translation across the weapons groupings. The first translation to be considered is to execute the technique using *espada y daga* (sword and dagger), with the *espada* (sword) held in a normal right grip and the *daga* (dagger) in a left normal grip. Assume a right stance to perform the defensive *estrella* movement, which travels from a middle right *abierta* origin to conclude in a middle right *serrada*

Estrella boklis using the short staff.

serrada ending. The *boklis* (upward diagonal strike) is executed using a rising back elbow strike to the pectoral muscles of the chest. The elbow strike travels from a middle right *serrada* position and travels diagonally upwards towards the centre line of the body.

A second opportunity to translate *estrella boklis* is to apply the move to an attempted right hand push at chest height. On this occasion the *estrella* (star block) is performed outside of the pushing arm and travels from a middle right *serrada* origin and concludes in a middle right *abierta* position. The star block is accompanied by a zoning step into left stance on the outside of the attacking arm. The *boklis* (upward diagonal strike) is in the form of a palm heel push under the chin and is supported with a left hand push to the lower back to knock the opponent off balance. The palm heel push travels from a low right *abierta* start and progresses towards a high right *serrada* conclusion.

Estrella boklis against a right shoulder grab.

abierta origin towards a middle right *serrada* conclusion. Maintaining blade alignment, the *estrella* finishes with the middle knuckles of the right hand pointing towards the rear to simulate a flat of the blade blocking motion. The second movement is *boklis* (upward diagonal strike), which travels from the middle right *serrada* position, towards the centre line and finishes at a target of the opponent's right armpit. The *boklis* strike leads with the middle knuckles of the right hand to ensure full structural stability during the striking motion.

Translation to Empty-Hand Applications

Estrella boklis is a deceptively effective technique that translates freely to empty-hand applications. The first application is used against a right shoulder grab with the first movement being a right hammer-fist strike to the biceps of the grabbing arm. The strike travels from a high right *abierta* origin towards a middle right

Estrella boklis against a right push attack.

GRANDMASTER EPIFANIO 'YULI' ROMO – THE CREATIVE GENIUS

Grandmaster Epifanio 'Yuli' Romo is widely acknowledged as the second most senior student of the late Grandmaster Antonio Ilustrisimo and is one of the 'Five Pillars' of the *Kali Ilustrisimo* system. A descendant of the respected Grandmaster Islao Romo, Grandmaster Yuli is heir to his family system as well as being heir to the rare *Borinaga Eskrima* system of Filipino Martial Arts. A very skilled fighter, Grandmaster Romo has trained many tournament champions in the Philippines. Grandmaster Yuli has travelled extensively throughout the Philippines is search of rare and effective forms of Filipino Martial Arts and it is the accumulation of decades of experience that has resulted in the conception of the *Bahad Zu'Bu* system. While retaining the core concepts, techniques and strategies of the *Kali Ilustrisimo* system, *Bahad Zu'Bu* is also a reflection of the creativity of Grandmaster Yuli Romo, as well as embracing the techniques and concepts of the Arts that form his life experience. A highly skilled and practical martial artist with a justified reputation as a leading exponent of explosive defensive strategies and disarming techniques, Grandmaster Yuli has spent many years working as a bodyguard and training armed forces personnel in the Philippines.

Grandmaster Epifanio 'Yuli' Romo.
(Photo: David Foggie)

Grandmaster Epifanio 'Yuli' Romo demonstrating blade methods. (Photo: David Foggie)

Kambal Abaniko – Twin Fan Strikes

The technique of *kambal abaniko* (twin fan strikes) is deceptively simple and yet a devastating method of switching tactics rapidly to strike alternate sides of the opponent. The name of this technique is very descriptive, with *kambal* meaning twin or double and *abaniko* meaning fan strike, and denotes two fan strikes in rapid succession aimed at targets on each side of the opponent. *Kambal abaniko* is very much a stand alone technique that is informed by the advanced *sinawali* (double weapon) method of *palis nakaw abaniko* (double parry with inside fan strike).

Structure and Mechanics

Kambal abaniko is a rapid method of striking towards targets on both sides of the opponent and involves two strikes often delivered in a horizontal plane to both sides of the opponent's head or neck area. An alternative could be to execute the strikes diagonally, from a low body height target to a high head level target, and for the purpose of this review the horizontal plane version will be considered. Starting from a right stance with the stick held in the right hand, the first strike travels across the body from right *abierta* (open) to right *serrada* (closed) at head height. In the first motion, the wrist is rotated to a palm up position and the strike leads with the middle knuckles to ensure blade alignment. The technique is

Kambal abaniko first move.

accompanied by a hip twist towards the left to generate maximum impact power. The right forearm is extended forwards to permit the blade accuracy to be maintained during execution and on impact with the target. The second strike is performed by reversing the motion in an anti-clockwise horizontal rotation above the head. The strike travels in a full circle through right *abierta* towards right *serrada* and finishes in a direction towards right *abierta*. Executed with a simultaneous right hip twist, the second strike leads with the middle knuckles to maintain structural competence and strikes to the opposite side of the head to the first strike.

Methods of Development

The execution of *kambal abaniko* requires excellent timing, range adjustment, considerable wrist strength and flexibility, speed and explosive impact power. A highly structured training methodology can greatly enhance the functional ability of this fast and devastating technique. The first solo training method is to perform *kambal abaniko* using a heavy metal bar. The technique should be performed extremely slowly

Kambal abaniko second move.

Kambal abaniko using a metal bar.

Kambal abaniko against the large diameter rope.

Kambal abaniko against the short staff.

Kambal abaniko against random attacks.

to enable the development of great strength and wrist flexibility throughout the motion, with minimal risk of wrist injury. It can be beneficial to follow metal bar training with a light rattan stick performance at a faster speed. This training method can improve wrist strength and flexibility greatly as well as augment speed of delivery.

The second solo training method that can improve speed and the development of explosive impact power is to strike a large diameter rope. Performance during this training method should be progressive in terms of speed of execution and degree of impact power, gradually increasing to full speed and power for both fan strikes.

The development of explosive impact power, speed and timing can be supported considerably by engagement with partner-based training. The first activity is to have the partner use a staff to present a target randomly for the execution of *kambal abaniko*. For maximum developmental benefits, this training method should be very mobile and dynamic and the staff can be presented for striking at any position above waist height. This method can greatly enhance the timing, accuracy and explosive impact power necessary to deliver this fast and devastating technique when under the full pressure of a combat scenario.

The second training method is to have the partner attack with single random strikes at any target. The defender can evade, block, parry or check the attack before using *kambal abaniko* as a fast and explosive counter-method. Greater benefit can be attained if the training partner is wearing protective gloves and a stick-fighting helmet to facilitate full speed and power in the delivery of the *kambal abaniko* counter-attack. Caution should be observed in any training method involving *kambal abaniko* because of the risk of wrist injuries.

Translation to Other Weapon Categories

Kambal abaniko is a fast and powerful method of the *solo baston* category that translates freely across the different weapon categories. The first option is to execute *kambal abaniko* using the *espada* (sword) held in a right normal grip and commencing from a high right *abierta* guard in a right stance. The first movement is to cut from the high right *abierta* origin towards the right *serrada* side of the body, turning the palm up and concluding at a head height target near to the centre line. It may be necessary to extend the right arm forwards slightly to facilitate an accurate cutting motion with the *espada*. The second cut travels anti-clockwise above the head, progressing through right *serrada* side, returning palm down towards the right *abierta* side and finishing at head height on the opposite side to the first cut.

The second option is to perform *kambal abaniko* using the *tungkod* (short staff). This very fast and destructive variation begins from a right stance with the *tungkod* held in a high right *abierta* guard and with the right hand palm up above the left hand, which is palm down. The first strike travels from the high right *abierta* start and moves inwards towards a high right

serrada position but concludes at head height with the right palm facing upwards and the tip of the staff close to the centre line. This strike leads with the middle right knuckles to ensure structural stability and blade alignment. The second strike reverses to circle anti-clockwise above the head, progressing through the high right *serrada* side and concluding at head height, striking towards right *abierta* but stopping close to the centre line and with the right palm facing down.

Translation to Empty-Hand Applications

Kambal abaniko is a technique that provides scope to strike rapidly towards both sides of the body in quick succession and translates well to the empty-hand category. One option can be to apply the move against an aggressive attempted grab with the right hand. The first movement is a painful limb destruction to the incoming arm using a right hammer fist technique that is delivered with the right palm up and travels from a high right *abierta* origin to a high right

Kambal abaniko using the sword.

Kambal abaniko using the short staff.

serrada conclusion. The second action is a right knife-hand strike to the neck and this motion begins in a high right *serrada* position and progresses towards the centre line with the right palm facing down.

A second application is to apply *kambal abaniko* at close range and as a redirection technique. The first movement is an inward palm slap to the face to shock the cranial nerves and this travels from a high right *abierta* position towards a high right *serrada* location but concludes on the centre line. The right hand then wraps around the head and then redirects the opponent as it travels from a high right *serrada* start and finishes in a high right *abierta* conclusion. A final two-handed push can divert the attacker and create enough distance to adopt escape strategies.

Kambal abaniko against a right grab.

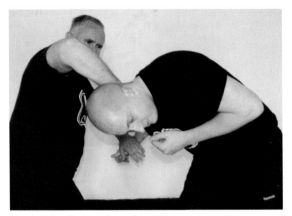

Kambal abaniko to redirect the opponent.

CHAPTER 5

INTERMEDIATE TECHNIQUES OF SOLO BASTON

Through progressive and consistent practice, the reward of enhanced skills and combative attributes is attained. This chapter will build on the fundamental *solo baston* (single stick) techniques to explore some of the more advanced concepts, strategies and methods of the intermediate single stick techniques of the Filipino martial arts. Scaffolding the fundamentals to build intermediate skills, the background, structure, development, translation and application of each technique is explored. Specifically, the chapter will review the techniques of high to low rebounding strikes with downward diagonal strike, wave thrust with vertical circular strike, thrust with circular strike, low parry with tunnel thrust and hooking parry with downward diagonal strike.

De Cuerdas Arriba Bagsak – High to Low Rebounding Strikes with Downward Diagonal Strike

A very fast, deceptive and destructive intermediate technique from the *solo baston* (single stick) category is *de cuerdas arriba bagsak* (high to low rebounding strikes with downward diagonal strike). The name of this technique is descriptive in that it indicates a high to low rebounding strike that is followed by a downward, diagonal finishing move. *De cuerdas arriba bagsak* is informed and influenced by the fundamental *solo baston* methods of *bagsak salok* (downward strike with thrust), *de cuerdas abajo* (low to high rebounding strikes) and *kambal abaniko* (twin fan strikes). In terms of target areas, *de cuerdas arriba bagsak* is influenced by the fundamental *sinawali* (double weapon) techniques of *magbabayo*

(downward X) and *salok-saboy* (upward X).

Structure and Mechanics

The core intermediate technique of *de cuerdas arriba bagsak* comprises three strikes that target three different corners of the body. Commencing from a left stance with the stick in the right hand, the first move is *nakaw abaniko* (inside fan strike) to the right side of the opponent's head. Often used as an *enganyo* (feint) technique, the first strike travels from right *abierta* (open) to right *serrada* (closed) by using an anti-clockwise rotation of the right wrist that results in the strike concluding towards right *abierta*. Reversing the motion of the first strike, the second strike is *boklis* (upward diagonal strike) that is aimed at the left hip or waist area of the opponent. This strike travels from right *abierta* towards the centre line in a right to left upward diagonal motion towards a waist height conclusion. The second strike then rebounds to

De cuerdas arriba bagsak first move.

De cuerdas arriba bagsak second move.

De cuerdas arriba bagsak third move.

a high right chamber in preparation for the third and final strike, which is *bagsak* (downward diagonal strike). The third strike is accompanied by a right step forwards into right stance and the strike travels from a high right *abierta* to a low right *serrada* position in a direct and powerful smashing motion.

Methods of Development

The progressive development of *de cuerdas arriba bagsak* demands a carefully structured approach to ensure that a highly effective combat-ready technique evolves. Solo training to develop this fast and aggressive move can include training with the metal bar to develop wrist strength and flexibility, speed and accuracy of motion. When training with the metal bar,

performance should be deliberately slow to afford some protection against wrist injury. Focusing on correct form with blade alignment is essential in this training method so that structural stability is maintained. The metal bar training should be followed by some light stick training, executing the technique at full speed to ensure that an explosive and functional *de cuerdas arriba bagsak* is achieved.

The second solo training method is to strike a large diameter rope using *de cuerdas arriba bagsak*. This training method helps to develop explosive impact power, speed, range adjustment, accuracy and a clear understanding of the potential of this destructive method. Training with the rope should build to full speed and power so that endurance is also enhanced. Structural stability, especially on impact, is paramount and each strike should lead with the middle knuckles to maintain blade alignment accurately during each strike.

Partner-based training methods are essential in the development of a fast and explosive *de cuerdas arriba*

De cuerdas arriba bagsak using a metal bar.

De cuerdas arriba bagsak against the large diameter rope.

De cuerdas arriba bagsak against the same technique.

De cuerdas arriba bagsak against random attacks.

delivery of *de cuerdas arriba bagsak* as a counter-striking method. Training with this method should be fast, dynamic and very mobile, and should focus on the development of excellent timing and range adjustment. This approach can be enhanced if the partner is wearing protective gear, including body armour and a helmet, to facilitate higher impact during delivery.

Translation to Other Weapon Categories

De cuerdas arriba bagsak translates fairly freely across weapon categories and the first translation is to perform the move using the *tungkod* (short staff). Starting from a left stance with the staff held at one end with the right palm up over the left palm down and chambered on the right side of the body, the first strike is *nakaw abaniko* (inside fan strike). The move travels in an anti-clockwise motion from right *abierta* through right *serrada* to conclude on the centre line at head height. Reversing the motion to travel in a clockwise trajectory, the second movement is a powerful *boklis* (upward diagonal strike) at hip height. This second strike snaps back to a high *abierta* chamber ready for the final *bagsak*, which is performed with a simultaneous stepping forward into a right stance. The *bagsak* travels from the high right *abierta* origin to conclude in a low right *serrada* position. It is important to maintain structural stability by leading with the middle right knuckles throughout the technique.

A second translation is to perform *de cuerdas arriba bagsak* using double sticks both held in a normal grip. In this method, the right stick is the dominant striking weapon. Begin in a left stance with both sticks chambered in a high *abierta* guard. The first motion is a simultaneous low left *palis* (parry) travelling from high left *abierta* to low left *serrada* while the right stick executes a high *nakaw abaniko* (inside fan strike) and both sticks travel in an anti-clockwise rotation towards their conclusion. Reversing the motion, the left stick performs *sima* (hooking parry), circling clockwise from low left *serrada*, across the centre line to end in a high left *serrada* position. At the same time, the right stick delivers a right *boklis* (upward diagonal strike) at hip height and travels from low right *abierta* towards the centre line. The final movement is *kambal bagsak*

bagsak. Training with a partner can greatly enhance the timing, accuracy, range adjustment and speed of delivery of *de cuerdas arriba bagsak*. The first partner-based training method is to have the partner perform the same technique and to strike his or her stick on each of the three strikes. This training method should be very mobile and fast in delivery and will help develop speed and accuracy against a moving target. Both partners should seek to maintain structural stability and blade alignment throughout the delivery of *de cuerdas arriba bagsak*.

The second partner-supported activity is to have the training partner feed with random strikes or thrusts, which can be blocked or parried prior to the

De cuerdas arriba bagsak using the short staff.

De cuerdas arriba bagsak using double sticks.

De cuerdas arriba bagsak to overwhelm the attacker.

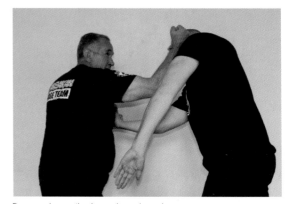

De cuerdas arriba bagsak to close the gap.

(twin downward diagonal strikes). Stepping into right stance, the left stick strikes first from high left *serrada* towards a conclusion at low left *abierta*. The right stick follows the same line, moving from high right *abierta* to conclude in a low right *serrada* position.

Translation to Empty-Hand Applications

De cuerdas arriba bagsak is a fast and dynamic method that translates well into empty-hand applications. One such option is used at close range and makes use of the direction of the first two movements of the technique. The move begins with a hair grab on the right side of the opponent's head. This initial movement travels across the body from the high right *abierta* reference point and concludes in a high right *serrada* location with the palm of the right hand facing right. The head is then pulled downwards towards a low right *abierta* conclusion and to meet the right knee that is driven towards the centre line of the body.

A second application of *de cuerdas arriba bagsak* is used when closing the gap from medium to close range. This adaptation makes use of the first two movements of the combination. The first attacking

motion is a right back-fist strike to the temple. The movement travels from a high right *serrada* start and progresses towards the centre line, smashing through the target to conclude in a middle right *abierta* position. The second move is a right palm up shovel punch to the mid-section and this technique travels in a forward direction from a low right *abierta* origin towards a middle centre line conclusion.

Tusok Alon Doblete – Wave Thrust with Vertical Circular Strike

A very fluid and effective intermediate level technique in *solo baston* (single stick) family is *tusok alon doblete* (wave thrust with vertical circular strike). The name of this move is indicative of waves crashing against the coastline and is suggestive of the destructive nature of this versatile technique. Tusok alon doblete is informed by and builds on the fundamental solo baston technique of planchada doblete (horizontal and vertical strikes) and in part has minor similarities to the intermediate sikwat lagusan (low parry with tunnel thrust). The technique further draws some influence from the advanced sinawali (double weapon) method of palis lagusan (double parry with tunnel thrust).

Structure and Mechanics

Tusok alon doblete is an excellent technique from the intermediate solo baston (single stick) grouping that consists of three techniques, which include a chest height thrust, a horizontal strike and a vertical strike. Starting from a right stance with the stick held in the right hand, the first move is a palm down thrust at chest level. This tusok (thrust) movement commences from a high right abierta (open) position with the palm of the right hand facing down and travels forwards and towards the serrada (closed) side of the body, concluding near to the abierta side of the centre line. The second movement, which is known as planchada (horizontal strike), is a palm up horizontal strike across the body at waist height. The strike travels from a middle height abierta origin to a full serrada position, also at waist height, and concludes by turning the palm down and with the stick pointing to the rear in a waist level serrada chamber. The second strike leads with the middle knuckles to ensure stability and blade alignment. The third move called doblete (vertical circular strike) travels forwards in a large clockwise circle and with vertical alignment towards a target at mid-section. The strike is performed fully on the serrada side but aims slightly towards the centre line of the body. The third strike leads with the middle knuckles for blade alignment and concludes by returning in a full circle to the waist high serrada chamber with the tip of the stick pointing to the rear.

Methods of Development

Tusok alon doblete is a technique that requires wrist strength and flexibility, speed and fluidity, timing, accuracy and excellent range adjustment. The first

Tusok alon doblete first move.

Tusok alon doblete second move.

TTusok alon doblete third move.

Tusok alon doblete facing a mirror.

Tusok alon doblete using a metal bar.

solo training method used to develop this technique is to perform *tusok alon doblete* in front of a mirror. This method should be used to correct and polish the fluid motions of *tusok alon doblete* and should be performed slowly throughout the three component techniques. Particular attention should be paid to the height variations and blade alignment, leading with the middle knuckles to enable a strong structure to evolve.

The second solo training method is to perform *tusok alon doblete* using the metal bar, with each component technique being executed very slowly to ensure that wrist strength and flexibility are developed fully. As with mirror training, using the metal bar should be viewed as a tool to develop accuracy throughout the technique. Caution should be observed during the delivery of the *planchada* (horizontal strike) and the *doblete* (vertical strike) as these require considerable wrist flexibility.

The development of excellent timing, range adjustment, speed and explosiveness can best be achieved through the use of partner-supported training methods. The first partner drill is to train in sparring mode, having the partner either block or parry the initial *tusok* (thrust) element of the *tusok alon doblete*. The *planchada doblete* (horizontal and vertical strikes) components can then be executed at speed as a countering method. This training method is most beneficial in a very mobile and dynamic context and can evolve with the *tusok* being used as an initial *enganyo* (feinting technique), drawing the block or parry and creating the opening for the continual motion into *planchada* (horizontal strike).

The second training method is to have the partner wear focus pads and present random targets for the thrust and striking motions. This should be done at speed and with great mobility so that accuracy and impact power develop against a moving target. In both partner-based training methods it is important to maintain blade alignment and structural stability by leading with the middle knuckles during the *planchada* and *doblete* movements.

Tusok alon doblete in sparring mode.

Tusok alon doblete against the focus pads.

Translation to Other Weapon Categories

Tusok alon doblete translates well across most weapon categories and the first translation is to use *espada y daga* (sword and dagger). Assume a right lead with the *espada* (sword) held in a right normal grip and the *daga* (dagger) held in a left normal grip. Checking with the dagger point upwards in a motion from left *abierta* towards middle left *serrada*, the first technique incorporates a simultaneous sword thrust at chest height, travelling from high right *abierta* towards a centre line target, with the palm facing down. The second motion includes a left *sima* (hooking parry)

travelling from high left *abierta* towards middle left *serrada* and above the sword, which executes a palm up *planchada* (horizontal cut), moving from middle right *abierta* towards a middle right *serrada* conclusion with the tip of the sword pointing to the rear. The final movement is to deliver *doblete* (vertical cut) with the *espada*, which circles forwards and downwards in a clockwise motion on the right *serrada* side, travelling from middle right *serrada*, towards the centre line and concluding in middle right *serrada* with the tip again pointing to the rear.

Another translation is to perform *tusok alon doblete* using the *tungkod* (short staff). Assume a right stance with the *tungkod* held at one end with the right hand with palm up over the left hand with palm down and in a right *abierta* chamber. The first move is to thrust the *tungkod* with the right palm down at a chest height centre line target, travelling from high right *abierta* towards high right *serrada* but concluding on centre. The second motion is a powerful horizontal strike at waist height with the right palm up and travelling from middle right *abierta* to conclude at middle right *serrada* with the right palm facing down and the tip of the *tungkod* facing to the rear. The final motion is *doblete* (circular strike) on the right *serrada* side of the body and aimed at a centre line target. This powerful strike travels clockwise on the right *serrada*

Tusok alon doblete using the sword and dagger.

Tusok alon doblete using the short staff.

side and returns to the origin with the *tungkod* tip facing the rear in a middle right *serrada* chamber.

Translation to Empty-Hand Applications

Tusok alon doblete is a fast and fluid motion that translates readily into empty-hand applications. One such option develops the strategic concept of ceasing the initiative during the encounter by switching tactics and uses the first two movements of the combination. The first begins in a left stance and makes use of a split

Tusok alon doblete to switch tactics.

Tusok alon doblete to unbalance and choke the attacker.

entry defensive motion against the incoming right arm. The left open hand parries the attack from a high left *abierta* position towards a high left *serrada*, ending at the same time as a right punch is delivered from a high right *abierta* guard towards a high centre line conclusion. At the point of contact, the right fist diverts horizontally into the biceps area of the attacking arm in a motion from the high centre line start towards a high right *serrada* finishing position, digging into the muscles with the middle right knuckles.

A second translation option makes use of the first two moves of *tusok alon doblete* to knock the opponent off balance and choke him or her. The defensive application begins in a left lead with a high guard position and uses a defensive shuffle diagonally forwards and to the left while executing a *sima* (hooking parry) to deflect the incoming right attack. The *sima* uses the back of the right hand and travels from the centre line towards a high right *abierta* conclusion. Passing over the top of the attacker's right arm, use a palm heel push to the chin to knock the attacker off balance. The move travels forwards from the high right *abierta* start and extends on the right *abierta* side of the body. The final motion is a choke technique applying horizontal pressure from the right *abierta* position towards a high right *serrada* finish and is accompanied by a left palm push to the lower back to knock the attacker further off balance.

Tusok Sing-Sing – Thrust with Circular Strike

Tusok sing-sing (thrust with circular strike) is a very fast and efficient method of countering a block or parry and is equally effective as an attacking combination of a thrust leading into an immediate circular strike. The descriptive name of this move indicates a thrust that is followed by a circular striking action. Conceptually informed by the advance *sinawali* (double weapon) technique of *pluma bukang liwayway* (pen defence with sun rays), this *solo baston* (single stick) method is almost a stand alone, but very useful, method. *Tusok sing-sing* partly informs the development of the advanced *putakti* (hornet) technique in the *solo baston* category.

Structure and Mechanics

Tusok sing-sing is an adaptable offensive or counter-offensive method made up of two movements, which includes a waist level thrust with an immediate circular strike. Starting from a right stance with the stick in the right hand, the first movement is a waist height thrust with the palm of the hand facing left. With the stick pointing forwards, the thrust travels from a low right *abierta* (open) position towards the centre line at waist height. The second movement is a circular strike on the outside of the body that returns to a target of the opponent's hand or arm. This motion, which is counter to a downward pressing block against the first thrust, is performed by the tip of the stick circling in an anti-clockwise rotation on the right side of the body and the strike makes impact upon the completion of a full circle. The rotation is performed fully on the *abierta* side of the body and is accompanied with a step back with the right foot into a left stance.

Methods of Development

Tusok sing-sing requires considerable wrist flexibility, speed, accuracy, enhanced range adjustment and excellent timing to use the technique effectively under the pressure of a combative scenario. The first solo training method to develop *tusok sing-sing* is to perform the movements using a metal bar. The technique should be performed very slowly and deliberately to ensure that good strength and wrist flexibility are achieved. The *sing-sing* (circular strike) motion should be performed accurately and finish with the middle knuckles leading to ensure that blade alignment is maintained. Metal bar training should be followed by a performance of *tusok sing-sing* using a lighter stick and at full combative speed for maximum overall development to be achieved.

The second solo training method is to perform *tusok sing-sing* against a horizontally aligned staff. This method requires great accuracy on the *tusok* (thrust) to hit the staff cleanly and then power can be developed on the *sing-sing* by striking the staff at maximum power during the circular motion of the

Tusok sing-sing first move.

Tusok sing-sing second move.

Tusok sing-sing using the metal bar.

Tusok sing-sing against a horizontal staff.

second move.

The necessary speed, timing, range adjustment, accuracy and explosiveness required to deliver *tusok sing-sing* are best developed during partner-based training sessions. The first partner-based training method is to use themed sparring with padded sticks. This method should be very dynamic with the purpose being for the partner to block or check the *tusok* (thrust) motion, which in turn initiates the rolling action into the *sing-sing* (circular strike). Training should be at full sparring intensity and can be developed further by using the *tusok* as an *enganyo* (feinting technique) to draw a reaction and create and

Tusok sing-sing using padded sticks.

Tusok sing-sing against the focus pads.

opportunity for the sing-sing strike to be delivered.

The second drill is to have the training partner use focus pads to present targets at random for the delivery of a fast and powerful *tusok sing-sing*. This training method should be very mobile and the emphasis should be on an initial fast, accurate and powerful *tusok*, followed immediately by a powerful *sing-sing* strike. The *sing-sing* motion should finish leading with the middle knuckles to ensure blade alignment and structural stability at the moment of impact with the target.

Translation to Other Weapon Categories

Tusok sing-sing is a fast and highly adaptable technique that translates freely to other weapon categories. The first translation is to perform the technique using *espada y daga* (sword and dagger) with the sword held in a right normal grip and the dagger held in a left normal grip. Begin the technique from a left stance with both weapons held in their respective *abierta* positions at middle height. The first motion is a simultaneous parry with the dagger moving from middle left *abierta* to middle left *serrada* while thrusting the sword to a middle centre line target travelling from a middle right *abierta* origin. Collectively this combination is known as *tulay* (bridge thrust). The second motion is a successive slash with the dagger moving from middle left serrada towards middle left *abierta*, and this is followed immediately by a *sing-sing* sword action, circling anti-clockwise on the right *abierta* side of the body to finish at a middle centre line conclusion and with the sword tip pointing forwards.

A second option for translating *tusok sing-sing* is to execute the move using the *tungkod* (short staff). Commence in a left stance and with the *tungkod* held on the right side of the body in a two-handed normal grip, right palm up above left palm down. Step forwards into a right stance and thrust the tip of the staff towards a central mid-section target. The technique travels from a middle right *abierta* origin to a conclusion on the centre line of the body. The second motion is to perform *sing-sing* (circular strike) by stepping back into left stance while circling the *tungkod* anti-clockwise on the right *abierta* side of the body and concluding tip forward towards the centre line and at a middle height.

Tusok sing-sing using the sword and dagger combination.

Tusok sing-sing using the short staff.

Tusok sing-sing against a wrist grab.

Tusok sing-sing to counter explosively at close range.

Translation to Empty-Hand Applications

Tusok sing-sing is a fast and explosive combination that can translate well into the empty-hand category. One option is to apply the move as an escape from a right on right wrist grab. First, allow the grabbed right arm to move forwards on the centre line towards the opponent. In a simultaneous action, perform a left palm slap to the attacker's right arm while retracting and freeing the grabbed right wrist. The slap travels down from a high left *serrada* origin towards a low centre line finish and the right arm retracts from the centre line towards a middle *abierta* position. Circle the right fist anti-clockwise on the right *abierta* side of the body and strike forwards with a hammer-fist strike, which travels from a high right *abierta* position to conclude at a high centre line target.

A second option to translate *tusok sing-sing* is to apply the move at close range and within the guard of the opponent. Commence from a right stance and deliver a fast right shovel punch to the abdomen region. The punch begins in a low right *abierta* position and finishes with the right palm facing upwards and on the centre line at a middle height. Circle the right hand anti-clockwise on the right *abierta* side of the body and finish with a hair grab that occurs in a high centre line location. Finally, pull the head downwards on to the centre line to meet a left uppercut punch, which is delivered on the centre line from a low left *abierta* origin.

Sikwat Lagusan – Low Parry with Tunnel Thrust

An important intermediate defensive technique within the *solo baston* (single stick) grouping, *sikwat lagusan* (low parry with tunnel thrust) provides a fast and fluid defence and counter-strategy, often executed while retreating or zoning to the side. The name of this technique is very descriptive in that it clearly conveys the tactics employed when performing the low-line parry and subsequent tunnel thrust. While partially informed by the advanced *sinawali* (double weapon) method of *palis palis lagusan* (double parry with tunnel thrust) and having minor similarities to the *solo baston* technique of *tusok alon* (wave thrust), *sikwat lagusan* is very much a stand alone, yet highly effective, defensive technique.

Structure and Mechanics

Sikwat lagusan is a retreating defensive strategic technique that consists of two movements and includes a stepping away low-line parry with a simultaneous alive hand check and stick thrust to the face or upper torso. Commencing from a right stance with the stick held in a high right *abierta* (open) guard position, the first move is a simultaneous step back with the right foot into a left stance while performing *sikwat* (low parry). The *sikwat* travels in an anti-clockwise motion from the high right *abierta* guard to travel across the body towards the right *serrada* (closed) side. The move crosses the centre line with the stick pointing downwards and then moving back to a low right *abierta*, completing with the stick still pointing down and brushing past the right knee and with the palm of the hand facing to the rear. The purpose of this motion is to engage and deflect a low leg strike. On completion of this motion, the left alive hand checks the attacker's hand, moving from middle left *abierta* towards a completion at a middle left *serrada* position. The stick is thrust simultaneously over the left checking hand, moving from right *abierta* towards the centre line at a target from head to stomach height.

Sikwat lagusan first move.

Sikwat lagusan second move.

Methods of Development

The development of *sikwat lagusan* requires excellent timing to execute the *sikwat* (low parry) with a simultaneous stepping away action. Further attributes that need development are wrist flexibility and strength, coordination, speed, fluidity, accuracy and impact power on the *lagusan* (tunnel thrust). Solo training to develop *sikwat lagusan* can include metal bar training, which should be performed very slowly to develop strength and wrist flexibility throughout the combination. Care should be taken to ensure that blade alignment is correct, while using the flat of the blade for the performance of *sikwat*, which is accompanied by a simultaneous stepping away motion with the lead foot. Greater improvements can be made if the performance using the metal bar is followed by a light stick execution at full speed and power.

The second important solo training method is to perform *sikwat lagusan* in front of a mirror to develop a refined awareness and accuracy of the two

Sikwat lagusan facing a mirror.

elements of the technique. This method should be deliberately slow and should greatly enhance the accuracy and fluidity of delivery. With practice, training should be done at full speed while using the mirror to support development.

The development of combative skills to enhance the delivery of *sikwat lagusan* requires a range of partner-based training methods. The first partner drill is to have the partner attack with low-line strikes or thrusts, which can be redirected or parried using the *sikwat* (low parry) technique. This training method should be mobile and dynamic, and the intensity should be gradually increased to full combat speed and power. This practice will improve considerably the timing, accuracy and range adjustment that are all required for the effective performance of *sikwat lagusan*.

The second training method requires the partner to use a stick and focus pad to feed random low-line strikes or thrusts while presenting the focus pad as a target for tunnel thrust. This training method should be dynamic and pressurized to encourage the timing and accuracy required to perform *sikwat lagusan* effectively in a combat situation. Both partner training methods should develop the accurate performance

Sikwat lagusan using the metal bar.

109

Sikwat lagusan against random low-line attacks.

their respective *abierta* chamber at middle height. The first movement is to execute the *sikwat* (low parry) with the right stick while simultaneously stepping back with the right foot into left stance. The parry travels with the tip of the stick pointing down and moves from a centre line intercept towards a low right *abierta* conclusion. Immediately, the left stick checks across the body, travelling from a middle left *abierta* origin to middle left *serrada* conclusion with the tip pointing upwards. Finally, the right stick is thrust from middle right *abierta* towards a centre line torso target, finishing with the palm of the right hand facing down.

Another option to translate *sikwat lagusan* is to perform the technique using the *tungkod* (short staff). Commence the technique in a right stance with the *tungkod* held at one end with the right palm up over the left palm down and the staff chambered in a middle right abierta guard. Step back with the right

Sikwat lagusan against a stick and focus pad.

of *sikwat lagusan*, ensuring the blade alignment is maintained while using the flat of the blade to perform the low parry.

Translation to Other Weapon Categories

Sikwat lagusan is a very practical combative method that translates freely across the weapons categories. The first translation is to perform *sikwat lagusan* using *doble baston* (double stick), commencing from a right stance and with both sticks held in normal grip and in

Sikwat lagusan using double sticks.

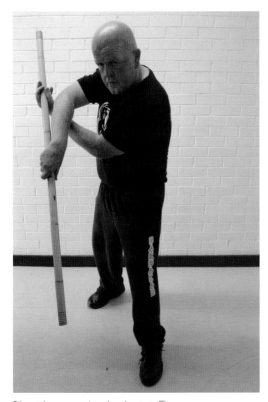

Sikwat lagusan using the short staff.

Sikwat lagusan against a wrist grab with counter-punch.

Sikwat lagusan against a wrist grab with takedown.

foot while executing the *sikwat* (low parry) with the tip of the *tungkod* facing down and the motion travelling from a centre line intercept towards a low right *abierta* conclusion. The second move is to perform the tunnel thrust, which travels from a middle right *abierta* origin towards a middle centre line target and is delivered with the right palm facing down.

Translation to Empty-Hand Applications

Sikwat lagusan is a fast defence and counter-movement that translates readily from *solo baston* (single stick) to empty-hand applications. The first application is to use the move against a strong right on right wrist grab. Step back with the right foot into a left stance and pull the right arm from the middle centre line grab location towards a low *abierta* conclusion. At the same time, push the attacker's right grabbing arm to the right to release the grip in a

motion that travels from a middle left *abierta* origin towards a middle left *serrada* conclusion. Maintaining the check on the attacker's right arm with the left hand, deliver a powerful cross punch to the face in a progression from a high right *abierta* start towards a high centre line ending.

Another application is to apply *sikwat lagusan* against a right on right wrist grab in a motion to offset the balance of the attacker and complete with a takedown technique. In a right stance, turn the grabbed right palm up to grab the attacker's right wrist from underneath. Step back into a left stance and execute an arm drag technique by applying pressure on the attacking elbow joint with the left

GRANDMASTER CHRISTOPHER 'TOPHER' RICKETTS – THE ARCHIVIST AND WARRIOR

Grandmaster Christopher 'Topher' Ricketts was one of the 'Five Pillars' of the *Kali Ilustrisimo* system, a founding member and Chief Instructor of the Bakbakan International organization. Additionally, Grandmaster Topher was the highest ranked Black Belt in the *Lameco Eskrima* system of the late Punong Guro Edar Sulite. Already a skilled and experienced full-contact fighter when he commenced training with the late Grandmaster Ilustrisimo, Grandmaster Topher was very instrumental and a key driving force in introducing regular full-contact sparring within the *Kali Ilustrisimo* group. It is a fitting testament to the

Grandmaster Christopher 'Topher' Ricketts demonstrating sword techniques. (Photo: Marissa Feliciano)

determination and drive of Grandmaster Topher that many of his students are respected for their fighting skills within the tournament arena. During over fifteen years of learning the *Kali Ilustrisimo* from 'Tatang,' Grandmaster Topher documented many hundreds of hours of footage of the respected Grandmaster in action. This archive is invaluable and has provided direction in the evolution of the *Kali Ilustrisimo* system as taught by Grandmaster Topher. A very respected exponent of the Filipino Martial Arts, a caring and devoted family man and generous friend, Grandmaster Topher passed away in October 2010 leaving the legacy of *Kali Ilustrisimo* in the capable hands of his sons, Punong Guro Bruce and Punong Guro Brandon.

Grandmaster Christopher 'Topher' Ricketts. (Photo: Beth Ricketts)

forearm in a motion from a high left *abierta* position and ending at a low left *serrada* location. Release the right wrist and return with a clothes line across the throat of the attacker in a movement that progresses from a middle right *abierta* start and travels as a straight arm swing towards a high right *serrada* conclusion. A slight push in the lower back with the left palm will assist the takedown action of the latter technique.

Sima Bagsak – Hooking Parry with Downward Diagonal Strike

Sima bagsak (hooking parry with downward diagonal strike) is another fast and destructive defensive method within the *solo baston* (single stick) category. The name of this technique is descriptive and conveys a high level hooking parry, which is followed immediately by a downward diagonal strike executed along the same line as the parry. *Sima bagsak* is informed strongly by and developed from the fundamental *solo baston* technique of *bagsak salok* (downward strike with thrust), and is effectively that sequence in reverse. The current technique informs the development of the advanced *sima bagsak*

Sima bagsak first move.

Sima bagsak second move.

salungat (hooking parry with opposite side downward diagonal strike) in the family of *solo baston* techniques.

Structure and Mechanics

As an intermediate technique from the *solo baston* category, *sima bagsak* is conceptually simple and yet it is a very important defensive technique. The technique begins from a right stance and with the stick held in the right hand and in a low right *serrada* (closed) chamber. The *sima* (hooking parry) is performed by thrusting the tip of the stick in an upward diagonal trajectory from a low right *serrada* origin to a high right *abierta* (open) conclusion, ending with the tip of the stick pointing to the rear and over the right shoulder. The motion is then reversed and the *bagsak* (downward diagonal strike) is executed from the high *abierta* conclusion of *sima* and travels in a downward diagonal path to a low right *serrada* conclusion. The strike leads with the middle knuckles to ensure that blade alignment is maintained and concludes with the tip of the stick pointing slightly upwards and towards the opponent. As the *baksak* is performed, it is accompanied by stepping back with the right foot into a left stance and with the hips twisted to the left to gain maximum structural power in the strike.

Methods of Development

Sima bagsak is simple in form but demands the development of advanced timing, accuracy, range adjustment and explosive destructive power to benefit fully from this destructive combative technique. The first solo training method is to perform the technique against a fixed staff. This training method can improve greatly the refinement of the correct angle for the *sima* (hooking parry), which can be followed immediately by a powerful *bagsak* (downward diagonal strike) technique. Correct blade alignment is essential to execute the *sima* using the back of the blade while the *bagsak* leads with the middle knuckles to ensure that structural stability is maintained.

The second solo training method to develop *sima bagsak* is to perform the moves very slowly using the metal bar. This method increases wrist strength and flexibility, both of which are essential for the fast and

113

Sima bagsak against a fixed staff.

Sima bagsak using the metal bar.

explosive delivery of *sima bagsak*. Metal bar training should be followed by performance of the technique using a light stick at full speed and power for excellent overall development.

The development of timing and accuracy of delivery can be greatly enhanced by the performance of *sima bagsak* during partner-based training. The first training method is to have the partner feed high level strikes or thrust attacks in a very mobile setting. This training method can improve significantly the timing needed to use *sima* (hooking parry) against a fast and powerful attack and the intensity of the attacks should be increased progressively as this timing develops. The *sima* should be performed accurately and blade

alignment maintained to facilitate the use of the back of the blade during the parry. Similarly, the *bagsak* is executed while leading with the middle knuckles to give strength to the technique and to preserve blade alignment.

The second training method requires the partner to use a stick and focus pad to provide random high-line attacks for the *sima* and a focus pad target for the execution of a fast and powerful *bagsak*. The intensity of attacks and degree of mobility should be increased gradually to a level of full combat focus. It is important that, even under the pressure and intensity of training, accuracy and structure are maintained throughout the performance of *sima bagsak*.

Sima bagsak against random high level attacks.

Sima bagsak against a stick and focus pad.

Translation to Other Weapon Categories

Sima bagsak is a combination technique that translates freely across a variety of weapon groupings. One effective translation is to deliver the technique using *doble baston* (double stick), with both sticks held in normal grip in a middle *abierta* chamber, with the sticks pointing upwards. In this translation the *sima* (hooking parry) is executed with one stick while the other stick performs the *bagsak* (downward diagonal strike) simultaneously. Commence in a left stance and perform *sima* with the left stick travelling from high left *abierta* towards a high left *serrada* conclusion, finishing over the right shoulder. At the same time, the right stick delivers *bagsak* that progresses from a right *abierta* origin towards a middle centre line finish and this strike leads with the middle right knuckles for structural stability and blade alignment.

The second interpretation into another weapon category is to perform *sima bagsak* using the *tungkod* (short staff). This powerful and aggressive combination begins in a right stance with the *tungkod* held at one end with the right palm up over the left palm down and in a low central chamber. The first motion is to execute *sima* (hooking parry), which travels from a low centre line origin in a hooking motion towards a high right *abierta* conclusion over the right shoulder. The *bagsak* is accompanied powerfully by a simultaneous stepping back into left stance and a left hip twist. The *tungkod* travels from the high right *abierta* origin in a downward diagonal motion that concludes in a low right *serrada* position.

Sima bagsak using double sticks.

Sima bagsak using the short staff.

Translation to Empty-Hand Applications

Sima bagsak is a fast combination method that translates freely into empty-hand applications. One such option is to apply the move against a right on right wrist grab. The first motion is to cup the opponent's elbow joint with the left palm to create a straight arm lock. Shift forwards and push the attacker's straight right arm upwards towards the shoulder joint to create an unbalancing action. In this motion, the right hand that has been grabbed pushes upwards in a direction from low right *abierta* towards a high right *serrada* position. Reversing the motion, remove the left elbow cup and place the left forearm palm down on the attacker's right elbow joint. Step back with the right foot into a deep left stance while dragging the attacker's right arm forcefully towards a low right *serrada* ending location. As the opponent's arm is dragged, rotate the left forearm to a left palm up position to assist in the impact of the drag.

Another option to translate *sima bagsak* can occur against an attempted right shoulder grab. Begin in a left stance and slip inside the incoming right arm while raising the left open hand from a middle centre line location to a conclusion in a high left *abierta* position and next to the left ear. Continue the forward motion to drive the left elbow into the opponent's right pectoral muscles in a spear action. Push the opponent with the right hand to create a slightly off balance position while smashing the left hammer-fist into the right collarbone. The hammer-fist travels from the high left *abierta* origin in a forwards and downwards arc towards a middle left *abierta* conclusion.

Sima bagsak against a wrist grab.

Sima bagsak against a shoulder grab.

CHAPTER 6

ADVANCED TECHNIQUES OF SOLO BASTON

The diligent and consistent practice of any combative technique leads to enhanced knowledge, understanding and the application of the more advanced methods within the chosen system. This chapter builds on the fundamental and intermediate techniques of *solo baston* (single stick) to provide a clear and detailed overview of some of the advanced techniques of single weapon training. The exploration will consider the background, structure and mechanics, development through solo and partner training, translation to other weapons categories and possible empty-hand interpretations of each technique. Explicitly, the chapter will consider the techniques of hooking parry with opposite side downward diagonal strike, cat eyes, star block with upward diagonal strike, outside fan strike and downward diagonal strike, hornet and comet with downward diagonal strike.

Sima Bagsak Salungat – Hooking Parry with Opposite Side Downward Diagonal Strike

Sima bagsak salungat (hooking parry with opposite side downward diagonal strike) is a strategically beneficial method from the advanced *solo baston* (single stick) category of the Filipino martial arts. The name of this move is descriptive and expresses the action of performing a high level *sima* (hooking parry) that continues into a downward diagonal strike on the opposite side of the body. Conceptually and strategically, *sima bagsak salungat* is informed heavily by the intermediate *solo baston* method of *sima bagsak*. The technique further informs the evolution

of defensive strategies in the form of another advanced method known as *matang pusa* (cat eyes).

Structure and Mechanics

While conceptually simple, *sima bagsak salungat* is advanced in application, timing and strategy. *Sima bagsak salungat* consists of two movements that quickly switch from a defensive to a counter-offensive strategy. This technique commences in a right stance

Sima bagsak salungat first move.

117

Sima bagsak salungat second move.

Methods of Development

The effective combat performance of *sima bagsak salungat* requires excellent speed, timing, wrist flexibility, coordination and explosive impact power. The first solo training method is to perform the technique in front of a mirror. Initially, the two movements of *sima bagsak salungat* should be performed deliberately slowly to ensure that a smooth and accurate delivery is achieved. This training method should improve greatly the coordination and wrist flexibility necessary for effective execution under the pressure of a combative scenario. It is important to ensure correct blade alignment so the back of the blade is used for the *sima* (hooking parry) and the cutting edge is leading on the *bagsak salungat* (opposite side downward diagonal strike).

The second solo training method is to perform *sima bagsak salungat* using a metal bar. This method will support the development of wrist strength and

Sima bagsak salungat facing a mirror.

with the stick in the right hand and held in a low right *serrada* (closed) guard and the tip of the stick pointing towards the opponent. The *sima* (hooking parry) is performed by thrusting the tip of the stick in an upward diagonal trajectory from a low right *serrada* origin to a high right *abierta* (open) conclusion, ending with the tip of the stick pointing to the rear and over the right shoulder. The second motion is *bagsak salungat* (opposite side downward diagonal strike) and requires that the stick is transferred to a high right *serrada* position, which is achieved in a looping action. The actual strike then begins from the high right *serrada* chamber and travels diagonally downwards to a low right *abierta* conclusion. The second movement is accompanied by a simultaneous stepping back with the right foot into a left stance. It is important that the second strike is performed by leading with the middle knuckles to ensure effective blade alignment and the structural stability of the movement.

Sima bagsak salungat using the metal bar.

Sima bagsak salungat against random high level attacks.

Sima bagsak salungat using double sticks.

flexibility, as well as improve speed of performance. Metal bar training should always be performed slowly and with the correct alignment and structure. This training method should be followed immediately by a performance of *sima bagsak salungat* using a light stick and at full combative speed.

To develop the necessary timing, speed and impact power to deliver *sima bagsak salungat* effectively, it is necessary to undergo extensive partner-based training. The first partner activity is to have the partner attack with random high level strikes to be defended against using *sima* (hooking parry), while presenting a focus pad target for the counter-strike using *bagsak salungat* (opposite side downward diagonal strike). For the best results, this training method will need to be very mobile and with the attacks gradually increased to full combat speed. Even

in the midst of pressure-testing the movements, it is essential to maintain structural stability and blade alignment by leading with the middle knuckles.

The second partner-based training method is to have the partner use double sticks to attack randomly with left or right high level strikes or thrusts. These will be defended against using *sima* and then a careful target can be selected for the counter-strike using *bagsak salungat*. This training method should increase gradually in terms of speed, mobility and the degree of intent in the attacks. Particular attention should be paid to correct form and structure, using the back of the blade for the *sima* and blade edge for the *bagsak salungat*.

Translation to Other Weapon Categories

Sima bagsak salungat is a deceptively effective method that can translate readily across weapon groupings. The first version is to deliver the technique using *espada y daga* (sword and dagger). Commence in a right stance with the sword held in a right normal grip and the dagger held in a left reverse grip. In this translation, the sword will execute the *sima* (hooking parry) while the dagger delivers the *bagsak salungat* (opposite side downward diagonal strike) in a simultaneous action. The *sima* travels from a middle centre line position towards a high right *abierta* conclusion, ending over the right shoulder. As the sima is executed the left dagger delivers a downward diagonal thrust travelling from left *abierta* towards the centre line and with a high to upper middle target.

Another option for translation is to perform *sima bagsak salungat* using the *tungkod* (short staff). This is a powerful and dynamic translation that begins in a right stance with the staff held at one end with the right palm up over the left palm down and in a low central guard. The *sima* (hooking parry) travels from a low centre line position and hooks upwards towards a high right *abierta* conclusion with the finishing point over the right shoulder. The *bagsak salungat* (opposite side downward diagonal strike) is delivered by looping the *tungkod* to a high right *serrada* position then stepping simultaneously back into left stance while striking diagonally down towards a low right *abierta* finish.

Translation to Empty-Hand Applications

Sima bagsak salungat is a fast and fluid movement that translates easily into empty-hand applications. One option is used at close range and begins with a right palm heel push on the opponent's chin in a motion

Sima bagsak salungat using the sword and dagger.

Sima bagsak salungat using the short staff.

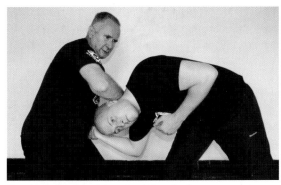

Sima bagsak salungat to redirect the attacker.

Sima bagsak salungat against a push attack.

from the middle level centre line towards a high right *abierta* location. Continue pushing the chin in an anti-clockwise rotation to spin the opponent as the right hand circles to a high right *serrada* position. Maintaining contact with the chin, grab the opponent's forehead with the left palm and step backwards to knock him or her off balance, then drag them to the floor in a direction from high right *serrada* towards a low right abierta conclusion.

The second opportunity to translate *sima bagsak salungat* to an empty-hand application is to apply the technique against a right hand push at chest height. Perform a right *sima* (hooking parry) to the outside of the attacking right arm by stepping left and forwards while raising the right arm from a middle centre line location towards a high right *abierta* location by the right ear in a motion to deflect the incoming push. Turn the right palm down to grab the attacker's right wrist and lower this to a middle right *abierta* position.

Simultaneously, place the left forearm on top of the attacker's right arm at the elbow and, in a motion from a middle left *serrada* origin towards a low left serrada conclusion, step back to knock the attacker off balance with a powerful arm drag technique.

Matang Pusa – Cat Eyes

Matang pusa is an advanced defensive method from the *solo baston* (single stick) that embraces switching of sides during the defensive manoeuvre. The name describes the cat eye shape of the path of the stick during the execution of the technique but is non-descriptive in terms of revealing the actual techniques used in this combination. *Matang pusa* is informed strongly by and derived from the fundamental *solo baston* methods of *estrella boklis* (star block with upward diagonal strike) and *bagsak salok* (downward diagonal strike with thrust). The technique is informed further by the motions of the advanced *solo baston* technique of *sima bagsak salungat* (hooking parry with opposite side downward diagonal strike).

Structure and Mechanics

Matang pusa is a strategically advantageous combination that can be used to switch rapidly from defensive to counter-offensive methods. The technique comprises four moves, namely *estrella* (star block), *boklis* (upward diagonal strike), *bagsak salungat* (opposite side downward diagonal strike) and *sima* (hooking parry). *Matang pusa* begins from a right stance with the stick held in the right hand and chambered in a high *abierta* (open) position. The first move is to perform *estrella serrada* (star block on the closed side) in which the stick travels from middle right *abierta* to middle right *serrada* (closed) and finishes with the middle knuckles pointing to the rear to simulate using the flat of the blade to block. The left alive hand checks over the top of the weapon hand in a palm down position. The second movement is *boklis* and this is performed by striking from low right *serrada* towards a high right *abierta* position. The strike leads with the middle knuckles to ensure that blade alignment and structural stability are maintained. As the *boklis* strike is performed, withdraw the right foot next to the left foot. At the pinnacle position, the *boklis* strike loops above the

Matang pusa first move.

Matang pusa second move.

Matang pusa third move.

Matang pusa fourth move.

head to begin the third strike *bagsak salungat* from a high right *serrada* origin, at which point step forwards with the left foot into a left stance. *Bagsak salungat* travels from a high right *serrada* position towards a low right *abierta* conclusion, leading with the middle knuckles to maintain blade alignment and finishing with the tip of the stick pointing towards the opponent's torso. The fourth and final technique in *matang pusa* is *sima*, which travels with the tip of the stick leading and commences from a low right *abierta* origin towards a high right *serrada* finish.

Methods of Development

The execution of *matang pusa* under the rigours and intensity of an aggressive attack demands the evolution of the highest levels of timing, wrist strength and flexibility, coordination, speed and explosive impact power. To enhance the necessary wrist strength, flexibility and coordination, the first solo training method is to perform *matang pusa* while using a metal bar. The nature of the wrist roll between the second and third motions requires that bar training is carried out very slowly and accurately. Correct alignment and structure are also essential elements when delivering the *boklis* (upward diagonal strike) and the subsequent *bagsak salungat* (opposite

side downward diagonal strike), and these are attained by leading with the middle knuckles.

The second solo training method is to strike a large diameter rope when using *matang pusa*. In this training method the first movement of *estrella* (star block) can be adapted as a striking motion using *bagsak* (downward diagonal strike). This technique, together with the subsequent *boklis* and *bagsak salungat*, should be executed with full speed and intensity to greatly enhance explosive impact power. It is essential that care is taken to maintain blade alignment and structural stability by leading with the middle knuckles of the weapon hand.

The development of timing, speed, wrist flexibility and impact power when performing *matang pusa* can be supported greatly by partner-based training methods. The first drill is to have the partner use a stick and focus pad, feeding a high level attack to be blocked or parried using *estrella* (star block) and presenting a focus pad target for the *boklis* (upward diagonal strike) and *bagsak salungat* (opposite side downward diagonal strike). This training method should increase gradually in intensity and mobility so that the delivery of *matang pusa* is eventually achieved in full combative mode. Care should be observed to ensure blade alignment and structural stability are maintained even under the pressure of an aggressive

Matang pusa using the metal bar.

The purpose is to defend using the *estrella* technique before launching an aggressive counter with the *boklis bagsak salungat sima* combination. The *sima* can readily be adapted to a *sunkite* (thrust) motion in the form of a powerful finishing technique. The best results will be achieved when this training method is very mobile and applied with combat pressure to ensure that correct and functional defences are developed.

Matang pusa against a stick and focus pad.

Matang pusa against the large diameter rope.

Matang pusa against random high level attacks.

assault.

The second training method is to have the partner attack with random high-line strikes or thrusts that originate from either the *abierta* or *serrada* position.

Translation to Other Weapon Categories

Matang pusa is a fast and destructive combination that translates well across different weapon categories. One option for translation is to execute the technique using *doble baston* (double stick) with both weapons held in a normal grip. The first motion begins from a right stance with both weapons chambered in their respective middle *abierta* guard positions. The right stick travels across the body from middle right *abierta* to a conclusion at middle right *serrada* and ends with the middle right knuckles facing the rear to finish the *estrella* (star block) technique. The left stick delivers *lagusan* (tunnel thrust) over the top of the right arm, travelling from left *abierta* towards a mid-section centre line target and with the left palm facing down. The second movement is to deliver a *boklis* (upward diagonal strike) with the right weapon travelling from low right *serrada* towards the centre line. At the same time, the left weapon performs a *bagsak* (downward diagonal strike) travelling from a high left *serrada* origin to conclude in a low left *abierta* position. Stepping back into left stance, the final combination movement is a left *bagsak* travelling from a high left *abierta* start towards a low left *serrada* finish. Simultaneously, the right stick delivers a *sima* (hooking parry) moving from low right *abierta* to end in a high left *serrada* position.

A further option for translation is to perform *matang pusa* using the *tungkod* (short staff). Start in a right stance with the *tungkod* held at one end with the right palm up over the left palm down. The first move is *estrella* (star block), which travels across the body from a middle right *abierta* origin to a middle right *serrada* conclusion with the middle right knuckles pointing to the rear. Immediately, deliver the *boklis* (upward diagonal strike), which travels from low right *serrada* towards high right *abierta*. The *boklis* motion loops around the head while stepping back into left stance to execute a *bagsak* (downward diagonal strike) that begins at high right *serrada* and concludes in a low right *abierta* position. The final motion is *sima* (hooking parry), which progresses from low right *abierta* to end in a high right *serrada* position.

Translation to Empty-Hand Applications

Matang pusa is a smooth and fluid advanced combination that can translate freely into the empty-hand category. One option makes use of the second

Matang pusa using double sticks.

Matang pusa using the short staff.

TULISAN – THE SCIENCE OF THE BLADE

Tulisan is the knife defence component of *Bakbakan Kali* that has been systematized by Grandmaster Reynaldo Galang. Heavily informed by the knife techniques, tactics and strategies of the late Grandmaster Antonio 'Tatang' Ilustrisimo, the Tulisan system provides a highly structured and progressive framework for the development and the evolution of skills against a bladed weapon encounter. Archived in *sayaw* (forms) and studied relentlessly against diverse and complex attacks, the methods of *tulisan* rapidly become instilled and an instinctive element of the practitioner's defensive arsenal. The methodology adopted when training in the *tulisan* system affords consistency, accessibility, progression and enhanced skills refinement. As a standalone system of defensive edged weapon strategies, *tulisan* is fast, simple, efficient, effective and very direct in approach and yet when used in conjunction with other weapon categories, such as *sinawali* (twin weapons) or *solo baston* (single stick), the skills of advanced *espada y daga* (sword and dagger) are revealed. Collectively the practitioner is able to develop a strong base for explosive middle and close range empty-hand techniques and strategies which can be applied against single or multiple attackers in a wide range of combative scenarios.

Grandmaster Reynaldo Galang, founder of the Tulisan Knife system. (Photo: David Foggie)

and third motions to bridge the gap and deliver a choke technique to the opponent. Against an incoming right hand attack, use *boklis* (upward diagonal strike) to deflect the arm in a motion that travels from a low right *serrada* position towards a high right *abierta* location. Shift forwards and to the left on the outside of the right attacking arm while passing the right forearm across the throat of the attacker in a motion from high right *abierta* to high right *serrada*. Finally, shift behind the attacker and push on the lower back with the left palm moving from a low left *abierta* origin towards the centre line. Pull inwards with the right forearm to complete the choke technique.

Matang pusa to bridge the gap.

Matang pusa against a right push.

A further opportunity to translate *matang pusa* is to apply the move at a medium range against an incoming right push. Slip inside the incoming right push and grab the wrist using the left hand in a palm out high left *abierta* position while executing a biceps destruction with the right hammer-fist travelling from a high right *abierta* position to conclude at a high right *serrada* point of contact with the attacking arm. Maintaining the left wrist grab, push upwards under the chin of the attacker with the right palm heel in a motion from middle right *serrada* towards high right *abierta* to knock the attacker off balance.

Estrella Boklis Abaniko Bagsak – Star Block with Upward Diagonal Strike, Outside Fan Strike and a Downward Diagonal Strike

Explosive in application, *estrella boklis abaniko bagsak* (star block with upward diagonal strike, outside fan strike and a downward diagonal strike) is a deceptively effective technique from the *solo baston* (single stick) category of the Filipino martial arts. The name of this advanced combination is very descriptive and clearly conveys the use of defensive star block, followed immediately by an upward cut, a fan strike and a downward diagonal finishing strike. *Estrella boklis abaniko bagsak* is strongly evolved from the fundamental *solo baston* methods of *estrella boklis* (star block with upward diagonal strike), *kambal abaniko* (twin fan strikes) and *bagsak salok* (downward diagonal strike with thrust). The technique is further influenced by the advanced techniques of *sima bagsak salungak* (hooking parry with opposite side downward diagonal strike) and *matang pusa* (cat eyes).

Structure and Mechanics

Estrella boklis abaniko bagsak is a very fast and aggressive method of switching from defensive to counter-offensive tactics. The technique consists of four movements that include *estrella* (star block), *boklis* (upward diagonal strike), *abaniko* (fan strike) and *bagsak* (downward diagonal strike), which allows for powerful counter-strikes aimed at different heights and sides of the body. *Estrella boklis abaniko bagsak* starts from a right stance with the stick held in the right hand and chambered in a high *abierta* (open) position. The first move is *estrella* on the right *serrada* (closed) side of the body. The star block travels from middle right *abierta* to middle right *serrada* and

Estrella boklis abaniko bagsak first move.

Estrella boklis abaniko bagsak second move.

Estrella boklis abaniko bagsak third move.

Estrella boklis abaniko bagsak fourth move.

finishes with the middle knuckles pointing to the rear to simulate using the flat of the blade to block. The left alive hand checks over the top of the weapon hand in a palm down position. The second move is a diagonal upward strike to the armpit of the opponent and this is performed by striking from low right *serrada* towards a high right *abierta* position. The strike leads with the middle knuckles to ensure that blade alignment and structural stability are maintained. The third technique is a high outside *abaniko* (fan strike) that circles in a clockwise diagonally upward motion from the mid-section *serrada* origin to a high section *abierta* conclusion. At the point of impact, the *abaniko* strike leads with the middle knuckles to ensure the stability of the motion and to maintain blade alignment. The final strike involves a simultaneous step back with the right foot into left stance while striking from a high *serrada* position to a low *abierta* ending. The point of impact is on the opposite side of the head to the *abaniko* strike and the *bagsak* leads with the middle knuckles to simulate blade orientation.

Methods of Development

Estrella boklis abaniko bagsak is a power defence and counter-method that demands the highest development of speed, accuracy, range adjustment, wrist strength and flexibility, coordination and explosive impact power to enable complete functionality during combat. The first, very effective method of solo training is to perform the technique in front of a mirror. This training method will greatly enhance the accuracy of delivery of *estrella boklis abaniko bagsak*, while further developing the necessary flexibility in the wrist for full speed and power execution. Mirror training should be performed slowly and with care to ensure that the correct blade alignment and structure are maintained throughout.

The second solo training method is to strike a large diameter rope using *estrella boklis abaniko bagsak*. This training method is outstanding for the development of wrist strength and flexibility, coordination and explosive impact power. Striking the rope should be progressive, building to full speed and power while still retaining the structure and blade alignment required for a combat-effective technique.

Training with a partner is the only effective way to

Estrella boklis abaniko bagsak facing a mirror.

Estrella boklis abaniko bagsak against the large diameter rope.

develop the necessary timing, accuracy and impact power when performing *estrella boklis abaniko bagsak*. The first training method is to have your partner use a *tungkod* (staff) to deliver high level attacks and present a striking target for the *boklis* (upward diagonal strike), *abaniko* (fan strike) and *bagsak* (downward diagonal strike). When performed with combat intensity and mobility, this training method will greatly enhance timing, accuracy, range adjustment and explosive impact power while maintaining a strong structure and blade alignment during each component technique.

The second training method is to have the partner wear focus pads to enable the development of full power attacks and aggressive defensive measures to be developed. The training partner should be very mobile and aggressive in presenting random targets, while the defender needs to maintain good form and alignment while executing the defensive techniques with full speed and power.

Translation to Other Weapon Categories

Estrella boklis abaniko bagsak translates readily to other weapon categories, especially the *sing* weapon groupings. The first translation is to use the *tungkod* (short staff) to execute the technique, which begins in a right stance. Holding the staff at one end with the right palm up over the left palm down, perform *estrella* (star block) that travels from a middle right *abierta* beginning position to conclude with the middle right knuckles pointing to the rear in a middle right *serrada* position. The next move is *boklis* (upward diagonal strike) aimed at the armpit and which travels from low right *serrada* towards the centre line. The third movement is *abaniko* (fan strike), which loops clockwise around the head to conclude in a high right *abierta* position. The final move is *bagsak* (downward diagonal strike), which travels from a high right *serrada* origin, concludes in a low right *abierta* location and is accompanied by stepping backwards into left stance.

Another single weapon translation is to perform *estrella boklis abaniko bagsak* using the *espada* (sword). Commence in a right stance with the sword held in a right normal grip and in a middle *abierta* chamber. Perform the *estrella* (star block) that travels from middle right *abierta* to middle right *serrada* and uses the flat of the blade at the point of contact. This is followed immediately by *boklis* (upward diagonal strike), which cuts from low right *serrada* towards the centre line and ends at the armpit of the opponent. Circle the *espada* clockwise around the head to deliver the third cut, which concludes in a high right *abierta* position. Stepping backwards into left stance, perform a *bagsak* (downward diagonal strike) that cuts from high right *serrada* and concludes at a low right *abierta* point.

Translation to Empty-Hand Applications

Estrella boklis abaniko bagsak is a fluid and powerful combination that can translate readily to the empty-hand category. One option is to use the *abierta*

Estrella boklis abaniko bagsak against the short staff.

Estrella boklis abaniko bagsak against focus pads.

version of the technique against a right aggressive push attack. Slip to the outside of the incoming right arm and use a right *estrella* (star block) to deflect the arm in a motion from the middle level centre line towards high right *abierta*. Once deflected, disengage the arm immediately and deliver a forceful right uppercut punch to the body in a direct movement from low right *abierta* to a centre line conclusion. Staying on the outside of the attacker's right arm, circle the right hand in an anti-clockwise direction to grab the right side of the attacker's head. Finally, pull the head downwards towards a low right *serrada* position to meet an upcoming right knee strike.

A further option can be to apply the last two movements of *estrella boklis abaniko bagsak* against a right on right wrist grab attack. Clasp the attacker's

Estrella boklis abaniko bagsak using the short staff.

Estrella boklis abaniko bagsak using the sword and dagger.

Estrella boklis abaniko bagsak against a push attack.

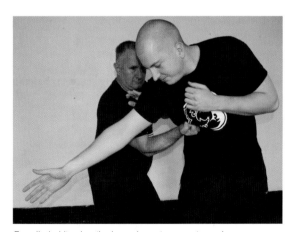

Estrella boklis abaniko bagsak against a wrist grab.

right hand with the left hand in a palm down position and rotate the right wrist immediately in a clockwise motion to grab the attacker's wrist from above. Step backwards and pull the attacker off balance and to the ground using an arm drag technique that travels from a middle right *serrada* origin towards a low right *abierta* conclusion.

Putakti – Hornet

Putaki (hornet) is a deceptively effective advanced combination method from the *solo baston* (single stick) grouping. The non-descriptive name of *putakti* conceals the hidden defensive and tactical essence of the technique, referring more to the 'sting in the tail' of the finishing third motion of *bagsak* (downward diagonal strike). *Putakti* is informed by the advanced *sinawali* (double weapon) of *luha redonda* (teardrop thrusts with whirlwind) and *luha salisi* (criss-cross thrusts). Further influences can be established by reviewing the fundamental *solo baston* methods of

bagsak salok (downward diagonal strike with thrust) and *kambal abaniko* (twin fan strikes).

Structure and Mechanics

A fast and explosive advanced technique from the *solo baston* category, *putakti* comprises three moves, which include a mid-section *tulay* (bridge thrust), *nakaw abaniko* (inside fan strike) and *bagsak* (downward diagonal strike). *Putakti* begins from a left stance with the stick held in the right hand in a low right *abierta* (open) chamber and the tip of the stick pointing forwards towards the opponent's abdomen region. The first motion is a bridge thrust which includes a simultaneous left alive hand parry, travelling from a high left *abierta* position in an inward arc to a low left *serrada* (closed) conclusion with the palm facing down. At the same time as the alive hand parry, the stick is thrust from the low *abierta* chamber towards the centre line at stomach height. Remaining in a left stance, the second movement is *nakaw abaniko,* which progresses from the mid-section

Putakti first move.   *Putakti second move.*   *Putakti third move.*

thrust in an anti-clockwise upward diagonal path, through the right *abierta* side and concludes in a high right *serrada* position at head height with the middle knuckles leading to maintain blade alignment. The final movement requires a simultaneous stepping forwards with the right foot into right stance while executing a powerful downward diagonal strike. This third strike is aimed at the opposite side of the head to the *nakaw abaniko* strike and travels from a high right *abierta* origin to finish at waist height in a low right *serrada* conclusion. The third strike leads with the middle knuckles to ensure that a blade orientation is achieved and structural stability is maintained.

Methods of Development

Putakti is a fast and aggressive combination that demands speed, mobility, wrist flexibility and explosive power to execute under pressure. The first solo training method is to perform *putaki* with a metal bar. This training method should be performed deliberately slowly and accurately, ensuring that the correct structure and alignment are maintained by leading with the middle knuckles on the *abaniko* (fan strike) and *bagsak* (downward diagonal strike) components of *putakti*. To develop speed in delivery, the metal bar training should be followed immediately by a performance at full speed using a light rattan stick.

Supporting the development of explosive impact power, the second training method is to perform *putakti* on a heavy bag. This method should increase gradually in speed, intensity and impact power while retaining correct form and structure. Grip strength during execution is especially important when performing the initial *tulay* (bridge thrust) on the heavy bag.

The development of combat timing, speed, coordination and impact power is best supported during practice by using a partner in a well-structured training session. The first training method is to have the partner act in a defensive mode and trying to block the initial *tulay* (bridge thrust) element of *putakti*, thus creating an opening for the *abaniko* (fan strike) and *bagsak* (downward diagonal strike) to end the confrontation. This training method can be greatly enhanced if the training partner is wearing protective equipment, such as a helmet, gloves and body armour

to facilitate the delivery of full power strikes during the encounter. Even at speed and under combative pressure, it is essential to lead with the middle knuckles during the abaniko and *bagsak* strikes to ensure that a good structure is maintained.

Putakti using the metal bar.

Putakti against the heavy bag.

The second partner drill is to have the partner feed high level strike attacks from either the *abierta* or *serrada* position. This method will enable the development and coordination of the alive hand parry or check element of the initial bridge thrust. The training session should be increased gradually in terms of speed, intensity and mobility and should facilitate a great understanding of how putakti may be used to create a range of openings during a combative exchange. It is essential to ensure that structural stability is not compromised during training by ensuring that blade alignment is maintained throughout performance.

Translation to Other Weapon Categories

Putakti is a fast and aggressive technique that translates freely across weapon categories. One option is to use *doble baston* (double stick) to execute *putakti*, which commences from a left stance and with both weapons held in a normal grip and chambered in their respective middle *abierta* guard positions. The first move is *tulay* (bridge thrust), which requires a left *palis* (parry) travelling from middle left *abierta* and concluding in middle left *serrada* with the stick pointing right. At the same time, the right stick executes a centre line thrust travelling from a middle right *abierta* origin with the right palm facing left. The second move is *palis nakaw abaniko* (parry with inside fan strike) with the left stick performing a parry from middle left *abierta* to middle left *serrada* while the right stick loops anti-clockwise to deliver the fan strike to a high right *serrada* target and is positioned over the left parrying arm. Stepping forwards into right stance, the final move is *sikwat bagsak* (low parry with downward diagonal strike) with the left stick performing *sikwat* (low parry), which travels from middle left *serrada* to low left *abierta* and concludes with the left stick pointing down. At the same time, the right stick delivers a *bagsak* (downward diagonal strike) travelling from a high right *abierta* origin and concluding at head height on centre line.

Putakti in defensive mode.

Putakti against high level random attacks.

Putakti using double sticks.

Putakti using the short staff.

A second translation option is to deliver *putakti* using the *tungkod* (short staff) in a fast and aggressive attacking action. Begin from a left stance with the *tungkod* held at one night with the right palm up over the left palm down and held in a middle right *abierta* chamber with the tip of the staff facing forwards. The first move is *tusok* (thrust), which begins in a middle right *abierta* position and travels towards a middle centre line target with the right palm facing left. Immediately, loop the staff anti-clockwise to deliver the *abaniko* (fan strike) technique to a target at a high right *serrada* position. Finally, step forwards into right stance to deliver a finishing *bagsak* (downward diagonal strike), which begins in a high right *abierta* position and concludes in a low right *serrada* location.

Putakti within a clinch scenario.

Translation to Empty-Hand Applications

Putakti is a fast and explosive combination that develops a range of generic attributes that transfer easily to the empty-hand grouping. One such option is to apply the technique at middle to close range within the guard of the opponent. In a clinch scenario, deliver an explosive right shovel punch to the abdomen of the opponent in a motion from a low right *abierta* point towards the centre line of the body. Grab the opponent's right wrist with the left hand while simultaneously grabbing the sight side of their head by reaching across the body to a high right *serrada* position. Finally, rotate both hands in a large clockwise direction to facilitate the delivery of the axil throw. The left hand moves from a middle left *abierta* location towards a high left *serrada* conclusion at the same time as the right hand travels from a high right *serrada* point, through a middle right *abierta* position and continues towards a low right *serrada* conclusion.

The second application to be considered is a very simple and direct defensive motion making use of the last movement of *putakti* against a middle right punch or knife thrust to the stomach. In a simultaneous action, deflect the incoming attack with the left hand travelling from a middle left *serrada* position towards a low left *abierta* conclusion. At the same time, the right hand executes a palm up knife-hand strike to the neck of the opponent in an action from a high right *abierta* origin towards a high centre line finish. If necessary, continue with a left cross, right uppercut, left cross combination to end the confrontation.

Putakti against a mid-section knife thrust.

Bulalakaw Bagsak – Comet with Downward Diagonal Strike

Bulalakaw bagsak (comet with downward diagonal strike) is a powerful attacking and counter-offensive technique within the *solo baston* (single stick) category. The name is partially descriptive in that it suggests a comet movement followed by a downward diagonal strike, but this does not convey the destructive application of this important and versatile technique. The technique is informed strongly by the *sinawali* (double weapon) methods of the Filipino martial arts, including the fundamental *magbabayo* (downward X) and *baguhan* (novice or C-shape), with further influences from the intermediate *bulalakaw* (comet) technique. Further links can be found with the *solo baston* methods of *bagsak salok* (downward diagonal strike with thrust) and *estella boklis* (star block with upward diagonal strike).

Structure and Mechanics

Bulalakaw bagsak is a very fast, aggressive and explosive attacking combination from the advanced *solo baston* (single stick) grouping. The technique contains three strikes that include a high inward strike, a low backhand strike and a finishing inward diagonal downward strike. Starting from a right stance with the stick held in the right hand in a high right *abierta* (open) chamber, the first move is a horizontal strike at head height. The strike begins in a high right *abierta* position, travelling inwards to conclude at a high right *serrada* (closed) position. The palm should be facing up and leading with the middle knuckles for blade alignment. The left alive hand is positioned in a high left *serrada* guard near to the right shoulder and above the right stick arm during the first strike. The stick now

travels in a downward anti-clockwise arc to begin the second strike from a low right *serrada* origin and this is accompanied by a clearing action with the left alive hand as it travels from high left *serrada* to high left *abierta*. The second strike is a horizontal movement beginning at the low right *serrada* start and ending at a low right *abierta*. This strike leads with the middle knuckles for blade alignment and with the palm facing down. The first two strikes are performed in a fast and smooth C-shaped trajectory before chambering in a high right *abierta* interim guard ready for the final finishing *bagsak* movement. A fast step forwards with the right foot supports the third *bagsak* strike, which travels from a high right *abierta* origin to a waist high right *serrada* conclusion. The move leads with the middle knuckles to ensure structural stability and blade alignment throughout this powerful finishing technique.

Methods of Development

Bulalakaw bagsak is a powerful and aggressive

Bulalakaw bagsak first move.

Bulalakaw bagsak second move.

Bulalakaw bagsak third move.

combination that requires well-honed speed, timing, wrist strength and flexibility, coordination and destructive impact power. The first solo training method is to execute *bulalakaw bagsak* with a metal bar to develop wrist strength and flexibility, grip strength, speed and coordination. When using a metal bar, the technique should be performed very slowly and leading with the middle knuckles in a bladed weapon format to ensure that good structure and alignment are maintained throughout. Metal bar training should be followed immediately by light stick training with the performance of *bulalakaw bagsak* being completed with full speed and power.

The second solo training method is to strike a large diameter rope using *bulalakaw bagsak*. Care should be taken to ensure that the correct striking range is maintained as well as accuracy of delivery with a strong structure and correct blade alignment on each of the three component strikes. When training to strike the large diameter rope, it is important to increase the speed, power and intensity of training gradually until full combat mode is attained.

The development of the advanced attributes of speed, coordination, timing and destructive impact power is best served through a structured approach to partner-based training. The first activity is to have the partner wear focus pads and present random targets for the three component strikes of *bulalakaw bagsak*. This training method, which also develops accuracy and range adjustment, should initially be performed fairly slowly and in a mobile context. Care should be taken not to strike the partner's forearms when executing the strikes with power. Gradually increase speed and intensity until full combat mode is achieved, while maintaining blade alignment and structural stability at full speed and power.

The second method is to have the training partner feed random high level strikes of thrust attacks, to be defended against using *bulalakaw bagsak*. In order to effectively apply this training method at the correct level, the training partner should wear full protective gear, including gloves, helmet and body armour to enable full power strikes to be delivered under the pressure of a combative scenario. It is extremely important to maintain blade alignment by leading with the middle knuckles during the delivery of each of the component strikes. This training method can greatly

increase endurance, speed, timing and the ability to execute *bulalakaw bagsak* in a combat situation.

Bulalakaw bagsak using the metal bar.

Bulalakaw bagsak using the large diameter rope.

Bulalakaw bagsak against the focus pads.

Bulalakaw bagsak against random high level attacks.

Translation to Other Weapon Categories

Bulalakaw bagsak is a deceptively simple and devastating technique that translates well across weapon groupings. The first option is to execute the technique using the *tungkod* (short staff). Begin in a right stance with the *tungkod* held at one end with the right palm up over the left palm down and chambered in a high right *abierta* position over the right shoulder. The first strike is a horizontal motion travelling from a high right *abierta* beginning to a high right *serrada* finish and is aimed at head height. The second strike is aimed at knee height and travels from a low right *serrada* position to conclude in a low right *abierta* position. The final strike is *bagsak* (downward diagonal strike), which is accompanied by stepping back with

the right foot into a left stance. The strike travels from a high right *abierta* location and travels to a low right *serrada* end with the tip of the *tungkod* pointing to the rear.

A further option for translation of *bulalakaw bagsak* is to use the *daga* (dagger) as a very fast and fluid combination technique. The technique begins in a right stance with the dagger held in a right normal grip and is chambered in a high right *abierta* guard with the tip of the blade pointing forwards and the right palm down. The first move is a high section horizontal slash with the right palm facing up and which travels from a high right *abierta* start to a high right *serrada* conclusion. The second motion is a middle palm down slash travelling from a middle right *serrada* origin to a middle right *abierta* finish. The final slash travels diagonally downwards from high right *abierta* to end in a low right *serrada* position.

Translation to Empty-Hand Applications

Bulalakaw bagsak is a fast and powerful technique from the *solo baston* (single stick) category that translates readily into a diverse range of empty-hand

Bulalakaw bagsak using the short staff.

circular motion, passing through a high right *serrada* position and continuing to a middle right *serrada* location before returning towards a middle right *abierta* finish. The action should be fast and fluid and redirects the head of the opponent towards their left side at waist height. The action can be finished with a double hand push in the lumbar region of the back to create distance and an opportunity for escape from the confrontation.

Bulalakaw bagsak using a dagger.

applications. One option can be applied against a right shoulder grab and makes use of the *bulalakaw* (comet) portion of the combination. As soon as the attacker grabs the right shoulder, immediately use a right palm distraction to slap the face in an inward motion travelling from a high right *abierta* origin towards a high *serrada* conclusion. Allow the right arm to pass over the attacker's right arm at the elbow joint in an anti-clockwise motion that returns from a low right *serrada* position towards a finish in a low right *abierta* location. The motion causes the attacker to be off balance and with a bent right arm. It can be completed by using the left hand to tip the nose backwards and facilitate a takedown technique.

Another option to apply *bulalakaw bagsak* is to use it to redirect the opponent at close range and from inside the guard in an unbalancing action. Slip inside the guard and immediately use the right palm to slap the left ear of the opponent in a movement from high left *abierta* towards a high centre line position. Grasp the head and continue in an anti-clockwise semi-

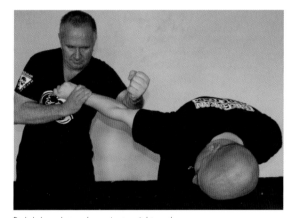

Bulalakaw bagsak against a right grab.

Bulalakaw bagsak to redirect the attacker.

CHAPTER 7

CONCLUSIONS

The conceptual nature of the Filipino martial arts affords both simplicity and complexity in development and comprehension. Techniques and training methods provide simplicity in that they are often categorized into weapons types, range or whether one or two weapons is being used. Yet beyond these simple classifications lie myriad opportunities to interpret, translate, adapt and apply in a seemingly endless variety of weapon and empty-hand scenarios. It is this complexity that has the potential to both confuse and stimulate interrogation, exploration and growth within the Filipino martial arts. An example can be found within the double weapon component common in most systems of the indigenous martial arts of the Philippines known as *sinawali* and trained with twin sticks or *doble baston*. It is vast and complex and can easily be interpreted and stand alone as a complete and devastating martial art. This book has provided a potential framework for exploration and discovery on the individual journey in the Filipino martial arts and yet this approach is far from complete or exhaustive, but merely an instrument to encourage and inspire ongoing evolution.

Creative Use of Equipment

Throughout the exploration of the Filipino martial arts it is apparent that the creative and thoughtful use of supportive equipment can enhance development and facilitate advanced skills and attributes. Sometimes readily available equipment is useful for supporting development while on other occasions the practitioner may need to make bespoke equipment to support his or her specific requirements. An example of such bespoke equipment is the striking frame, which is a wooden square perimeter with the two diagonal components fitted from corner to corner to create an X shape within the frame. When fixed to a wall this equipment has several applications, the first of which is as a visual aid to support accurate horizontal, vertical and diagonal striking patterns. The striking frame also supports the accurate use of the tip when striking in fast combinations against a solid target, such as when training *de cuerdas arriba bagsak* (high to low rebounding strikes with downward diagonal strike) or *planchada doblete* (horizontal and vertical strikes), both of which require very accurate range adjustment during execution. A further opportunity to use the striking frame is when practising striking methods that impact on more than one target in a single motion, or that immediately revert to another target after the initial impacting strike. Striking two components of the frame could simulate a *bagsak* (downward diagonal strike) strike hitting the head then the hands in one motion. Another option could

Using the striking frame.

be striking one component of the frame with a single *bagsak* strike then thrusting to another component with the *salok* (scooping thrust) conclusion to represent a hand strike and a thrust to the body or face.

Innovation in Weapons Training

Regardless of which weapon or combination of weapons is being practised, once the basic motions are fluid and well understood there are considerable opportunities for innovation and enhanced development. An example of this occurs when using the stick in the *susi* (key or reverse) grip to deliver such techniques as *magbabayo* (downward X), *salok saboy* (upward X) or *redonda* (whirlwind). The feel, fluidity and delivery of such techniques totally alters and can feel awkward and barely effective, yet this grip is common when using a walking stick, for example. Adaptations, such as the realignment of the body, can greatly improve performance and effectiveness. The sticks developed through practising and developing skills in using the reverse grip can then lead to advanced weapon combination strategies, such as *kalis kaluban* (sword and scabbard) techniques.

Advanced weapon combinations.

Using the stick in reverse grip.

The practitioner of the Filipino martial arts has many options when using a diversity of weapons that are readily available. It is essential to fully understand, appreciate and adapt to the different weapon categories and how these variants respond during and after the delivery of a strike, cut or thrust. One category that offers great scope for exploration, analysis and evaluation is that of the flexible weapons because this group responds very differently to the right stick and blade options. Training with the *tabak toyok* (flails) provides excellent opportunities to understand how to adapt standard stick techniques to match the unpredictable character of flexible weapons and to provide clarity on which stick weapons are potentially unsafe to the practitioner. Techniques such as *magbabayo* (downward X) or *planchada doblete* (horizontal and vertical strikes) can be applied readily with the *tabak toyok* with minimal adaptation. Other methods such as *de cuerdas abajo* (low to high rebounding strikes) would depend on the nature of the rebound from the first strike, thus injecting a strong element of uncertainty that could lead to the failed delivery of the technique.

Using flexible weapons.

Adaptive Empty-Hand Development

While there is a misconception that the Filipino martial arts lack empty-hand skills, careful thought, analysis and creativity can lead to a devastating ability in this less obvious component. One such option for exploration is to follow the lines of the stick techniques to provide scope for a range of empty-hand methods. At a basic level, the lines traced during the performance of *salok saboy* (upward X) could simply translate to two uppercut punches or two diagonally rising elbow strikes using alternate arms. Similarly, the line of *planchada* (horizontal strike) could simply be a mid-section hook punch and *abaniko* provides the lines for alternate high hook punches. With progressive and creative adaptation, more advanced empty-hand methods can evolve, such as following the striking lines of *de cuerdas arriba bagsak* (high to low rebounding strikes with downward diagonal strike). This could readily be interpreted as a

PANGAMUT – DEVASTATING EMPTY HANDS

Pangamut is a term often used to describe the empty hand component of the Filipino martial arts and is sometimes simply defined as Filipino Boxing. Dispelling the misconception that the Filipino martial arts are 'good with weapons but not effective with empty hands', *pangamut* is a unique blend of *suntok* (punches), *sipa* (kicks), *tuhod* (knees) and *siko* (elbows). Additionally, *pangamut* embraces such methods as *ulo hangganan* (head-butting), *gunting* (limb or muscle destructive strikes) and *dumog* (grappling). Many techniques of *pangamut* are a direct evolution of the *armas* (arms) or *sandata* (weapons) component of the Filipino martial arts. Informed and developed by the devastating stick and blade methods of *arnis*, *eskrima* or *kali* (generic terms for the Filipino martial arts), the practitioner is equipped with the ability to flow freely between weapon-based and empty hand combat ranges. Techniques from the *baraw* (dagger) evolve into elbow strikes and punches, while methods of *sinawali* (double weapons) readily adapt into explosive entry methods, joint locks or throwing techniques. Through constant practice and exploring the depths of the Filipino martial arts, many unique and highly effective empty hand methods are revealed and evolve.

Reynaldo Galang demonstrating a throwing technique. (Photo: David Foggie)

De cuerdas arriba bagsak second strike.

Punching along the line of stick strikes.

Analysis of hand positions.

De cuerdas abajo first strike.

diagonal strike) easily relations to the directional motion of an arm dragging technique.

Another approach to exploring the relationship between weapons and empty-hand techniques is to analyze hand positions at different points of the motion. An example could be to review the hand positions of the *sinawali* (double weapon) technique of *de cuerdas* (rebounding strikes). The first motion not only provides a translation to a shovel punch or uppercut punch, but opportunities for a finger lock, wrist lock, leg lock, shoulder lock, choke, strangle, neck crank and a variety of throwing methods. Similarly, a review of the hand positions of the *putakti* (hornet) technique can identify close range striking into the axil throw technique as well as a range of locking and choking methods. It is the ability to explore opportunities beyond the obvious weapon technique that truly reveals the endless empty-handed scope of the devastating Filipino martial arts.

The scope for exploration, analysis and evaluation of the techniques associated with the Filipino martial arts is vast and can be daunting to the practitioner. In many ways the opportunity to fully engage in such activities is largely individual and limited only by the openness of mind and the sense of personal creativity. The search beyond the obvious physical attributes of the techniques studied is challenging, sometimes frustrating but always extremely rewarding. Enjoy the journey!

high hook punch, into a mid-section shovel punch and concluding with a downward diagonal punch or an explosive three-strike elbow combination. The striking lines may also provide opportunities for locking or grappling techniques, such as *bagsak* (downward

FURTHER READING

While not an exhaustive bibliography, the following details provide opportunities for further exploration of the Filipino martial arts:

Baron Saguin, Peachie, *Punta y Daga of Kalis Ilustrisimo* (Manila, Baron Saguin, 2014)

Diego, Antonio and Ricketts, Christopher, *The Secrets of Kalis Ilustrisimo* (Rutland, Vermont: Charles E. Tuttle Co, 2002)

Galang, Reynaldo S., *Classic Arnis: The Legacy of Placido Yambao* (New Jersey: Arjee Enterprises, 2004)

Galang, Reynaldo S., *Complete Sinawali: Filipino Double Weapon Fighting* (North Clarendon: Tuttle Publishing, 2000)

Galang, Reynaldo S., *Masters of the Blade* (New Jersey: Arjee Enterprises, 2006)

Galang, Reynaldo S., *Warrior Arts of the Philippines* (New Jersey: Bakbakan International, 2006)

Wiley, Mark V., *Arnis: History and Methods of Filipino Martial Arts* (Rutland, Vermont: Charles E. Tuttle Co, 2001)

Wiley, Mark V., *Filipino Martial Arts* (California, Unique Publications, 2001)

Wiley, Mark V., *Filipino Martial Culture* (Rutland, Vermont: Charles E. Tuttle Co, 1997)

GLOSSARY

Abaniko Fan strike
Abierta Open position
Anggulo Angles of attack
Arnis A name of the Filipino martial arts
Arnis de Mano A name of the Filipino martial arts
Baguhan Novice – C-shaped strikes
Bagsak Downward diagonal strike
Bagsak salok Downward strike with thrust
Bagsak salungat Downward strike on the opposite side
Bahi A Filipino hardwood
Balisong A folding knife
Banday-kamay Guardian hand
Baraw A type of knife
Barong A leaf-shaped sword
Barya Coin
Baston Rattan cane
Bato Stone or rock
Boklis Diagonal upward strike
Bukang Liwayway Sun rays
Bulalakaw Comet
Daga Dagger
De cuerdas Rebounding strikes
Doble baston Double rattan canes
Doblete Vertical circular strike
Dulo-dulo A short palm stick
Escrima A name of the Filipino martial arts
Eskrima A name of the Filipino martial arts
Espada Sword
Espada y daga Sword and dagger
Estrella Star block
Ginungting A type of Filipino sword
Kadena Chain
Kali A name of the Filipino martial arts

Kamagong Filipino iron wood
Kambal Twin
Kampilan A type of Filipino sword
Kerambit A short hook-shaped knife
Lagusan Tunnel
Lubid Rope
Luha redonda Teardrop thrusts with whirlwind
Luha salisi Criss-cross thrusts
Magbabayo To pound – downward X
Matang pusa Cat eyes
Pagkilos Movement or motion
Palis Parry
Pana Bow
Panyo Handkerchief
Planchada Horizontal strike
Pluma Pen
Putakti Hornet
Redonda Whirlwind
Redonda salok-saboy Reverse whirlwind
Salok-saboy Scoop and throw – upward X
Sansibar A type of Filipino sword
Sibat Spear
Siit Twig
Sikwat A low parry
Sima A hooking parry
Sinawali Twin weapons art
Sing-sing Ring or circle
Solo baston Single cane
Tabak toyok Flails
Tirador Slingshot
Tiyempo Timing
Tulay Bridge
Tungkod Staff

INDEX